Seed Sounds for
Tuning the Chakras

"As sound pioneer, concert musician, music philosopher, and conduit of the perennial wisdom, James D'Angelo is a refreshingly original communicator. Ever since I first heard him, 25 years ago, enchant his audience with a thoroughly engaging presentation of sound healing, I realized that here is a man who walks his talk. James's passionate, humble, humorous, and scholarly dedication to the transforming art of sound and voice is celebrated on every page of *Seed Sounds for Tuning the Chakras*. It's a spiritual adventure with your voice, with an inventive range of vocal exercises—accessible for everyone—that are both playful and profound. I encourage all my voice students and friends dedicated to the evolution of consciousness through sound to discover the healing properties of *Seed Sounds for Tuning the Chakras*."

CHLOE GOODCHILD, FOUNDER OF
THE NAKED VOICE FOUNDATION AND TRAINING PROGRAM
AND AUTHOR OF *THE NAKED VOICE*

"James D'Angelo has created an intriguing journey into the realm of using self-created sounds for healing and transformation. Well written and finely researched, this book features unique material on the creative sources of sound, as well as exercises and recorded examples on how to apply this information. *Seed Sounds for Tuning the Chakras* is a fine addition to the library of anyone interested in this fascinating subject."

JONATHAN GOLDMAN, AUTHOR OF
CHAKRA FREQUENCIES AND *HEALING SOUNDS* AND
DIRECTOR OF THE SOUND HEALERS ASSOCIATION

"James D'Angelo's *Seed Sounds for Tuning the Chakras* is an excellent resource for exploring fundamental methodology of using voice for toning exercises and chakra attunements. James's manner of explaining the background and method of working with the chakras is a pleasing mix of traditional wisdom and contemporary insight. His introduction includes an exceptional, concise treatise on the nature of human existence and an endearing exploration into the interrelationship between sound and matter, name and form, across traditions. His wordplay while naming chakra characteristics is insightful and articulate. His accompanying CD adequately demonstrates the many vowel, consonant, breath, and seed sounds he utilizes in his many explanations and exercises."

ZACCIAH BLACKBURN, PH.D.,
DIRECTOR OF THE CENTER OF LIGHT INSTITUTE OF
SOUND HEALING AND SHAMANIC STUDIES AND
DIRECTOR OF EDUCATION AT THE INTERNATIONAL
SOUND HEALING NETWORK

SEED SOUNDS FOR TUNING THE CHAKRAS

Vowels, Consonants, and Syllables for Spiritual Transformation

James D'Angelo, Ph.D.

DESTINY BOOKS

Destiny Books
Rochester, Vermont • Toronto, Canada

Destiny Books
One Park Street
Rochester, Vermont 05767
www.DestinyBooks.com

SUSTAINABLE FORESTRY INITIATIVE

Certified Sourcing
www.sfiprogram.org
SFI-00854

Text stock is SFI certified

Destiny Books is a division of Inner Traditions International

Library of Congress Cataloging-in-Publication Data

D'Angelo, James.
  Seed sounds for tuning the chakras : vowels, consonants, and syllables for spiritual transformation / James D'Angelo.
    p. cm.
  Includes bibliographical references and index.
  ISBN 978-1-59477-460-7 (pbk.) — ISBN 978-1-62055-002-1 (e-book)
  1. Music therapy. 2. Sound—Psychological aspects. 3. Chakras. I. Title.
ML3920.D25 2012
615.8′5154—dc23

2012005193

Printed and bound in the United States by Lake Book Manufacturing, Inc. The text stock is SFI certified. The Sustainable Forestry Initiative® program promotes sustainable forest management.

10 9 8 7 6 5 4 3 2 1

Text design by Virginia Scott-Bowman and layout by Jack Nichols
This book was typeset in Garamond Premier Pro with Warnock Pro and Gill Sans Pro used as display typefaces.

To send correspondence to the author of this book, mail a first-class letter to the author c/o Inner Traditions • Bear & Company, One Park Street, Rochester, VT 05767, and we will forward the communication, or contact the author directly at **www.soundspirit.co.uk.**

Dedicated to the memory of

His Holiness Shantanand Saraswati (1913–1997),

formerly the Shankaracharya of North India (1953–1980),

from whom I received spiritual knowledge that has subtly

contributed to the writing of this book.

Somewhere deep inside there is a sound that is mine alone, and I struggle daily to hear it and tune my life to it.

RACHEL NAOMI REMEN,
MY GRANDFATHER'S BLESSINGS

Contents

❀

Acknowledgments

My thanks to Georgina D'Angelo for all her help in proofreading and editing of this book. Thanks also to those who have inspired me by their work in the holistic healing field: Don Campbell, Michael Deason-Barrow, Christopher Gibbs, Jonathan Goldman, Gabriele Gschwendtner, Chloe Goodchild, Susan Hale, Andrew Hodges, Reuben Kay, Margaret Koolman, Fabien Maman, Solveig McIntosh, Dale Pond, and Frank Perry.

INTRODUCTION
The Spiritual Path

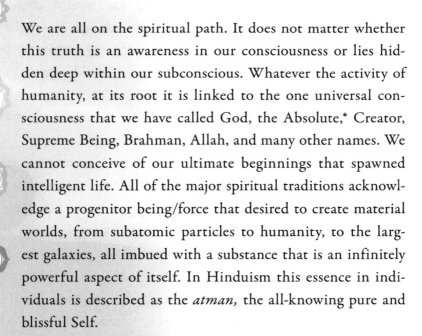

We are all on the spiritual path. It does not matter whether this truth is an awareness in our consciousness or lies hidden deep within our subconscious. Whatever the activity of humanity, at its root it is linked to the one universal consciousness that we have called God, the Absolute,* Creator, Supreme Being, Brahman, Allah, and many other names. We cannot conceive of our ultimate beginnings that spawned intelligent life. All of the major spiritual traditions acknowledge a progenitor being/force that desired to create material worlds, from subatomic particles to humanity, to the largest galaxies, all imbued with a substance that is an infinitely powerful aspect of itself. In Hinduism this essence in individuals is described as the *atman,* the all-knowing pure and blissful Self.

What is the nature of this Creation? With the exception of ourselves, all expresses order and harmony, and Creation is

---

*The word *Absolute* is perhaps the best English term to denote what is usually given as God. It begins with the first letter of the alphabet and could be connected to *absolution,* the forgiveness of the Absolute for humanity's forgetting who they really are.

1

unfolding as intended.* Even events considered to be disastrous, such as earthquakes and erupting volcanoes, are part of that order and harmony. They are the Earth's way of renewing and cleansing itself. The aspect of Creation that has not attained this harmony is our psychology, the life of the soul. The Absolute did not establish a world of human perfection in which our mind states and our overall health would not go astray. Rather, it took on the role of a cosmic dramatist by not programming sentient beings, but giving them the choice of remembering that their knowing union with the Absolute is the source of harmony, peace, and bliss. This is the primary paradox, and paradox is part of the spiritual path. It is paradoxical because the Absolute would know that humanity would forget its existence, but give us the means of finding the way back. This is the greatest drama there is.

Each of us is endowed with a soul, the center point of which, according to Hindu theology, lies between the heart and the throat. It is our inner organ that determines to what extent we are reflecting our divine essence or, conversely, acting as a separate, independent creature with its own power to do as it pleases. The purer its nature, the more the soul can guide us into a state of unconditional happiness where the heart is fully open and the mind quiet. It is a condition without cause and the most healing state we can achieve. It is as though we have tuned into a different frequency, a much finer vibration of another dimension.

---

*A wonderful example of nature being in harmony can be heard on a recording called God's Chorus of Crickets. Composer Jim Wilson slowed way down a recording of cricket sounds, and extended the vibrations. The result is reminiscent of an ethereal, angelic choir.

Any distortions in the soul's frequencies are the result of all the experiences it has accumulated in its journey through many lives. The identification with the material world with its myriad events and conflicting emotions becomes ever greater, functioning almost as a prison. Yet the soul's underlying desire is to have conscious reunification with the Absolute. It is summarized in the dictum, "*In this world but not of this world.*" Herein lies another paradox.

So each of us is a noncorporeal soul dwelling temporarily in a physical body with all its senses. The soul's frequencies are distorted, literally out of tune, because it has lost its way due to the domination of the senses and the discursive mind. These disturbances, which need to be healed, are first experienced in our psychology, and this has consequences at both the physical and spiritual levels. Whatever path we choose to return to the source of our being, it is ultimately about the healing of the soul. *Healing* is the operative word as opposed to *curing*. Healing—to make whole—is directed toward the finer aspects of our nature and alters our psychology for the better. This often carries over into the physical body. The pathway toward this healing is usually threefold: Receiving spiritual knowledge from self-realized teachers, whether through the spoken or written word; living that knowledge that has imprinted itself on our consciousness; and establishing practices and rituals that awaken and purify our soul life.

The purpose of this book is to provide one of these ritual pathways via awakening and resonating to the innate vibratory powers of vowels, consonants, and seed syllables for transformation and healing. By investing them with meaning we can then consciously use them to re-tune and purify our energy centers—our *chakras,* an integral part of the soul. Our voices, the master instruments for producing rich, natural sounds, can lead us toward the source of our being, enabling us to integrate and become one with the voice of the Absolute. This is the union, or yoga, that the soul deeply desires, and our voices can be the conduit to this blissful paradise.

1
Creation as Vibration

In the beginning was the Word, and the Word was with God, and the Word was God. The same was in the beginning with God. All things were made by him, and without him was not any thing made that was made. In him was life and the life was the light of men. And the light shone in the darkness and the darkness did not overcome it.

The Logos existed in the very beginning. The Logos was with God, the Logos was Divine. It was with God in the very beginning. Through the Logos all existence came into being, no existence came into being apart from the Logos. In it life lay, and this life was the light of humanity; amid the darkness the light shone and the darkness did not master it.

These two versions of the opening verses of St. John's Gospel (John 1: 1–5) proclaim that the whole of Creation came into existence through a singular all-powerful vibration. Into the void of space was projected the voice of the Absolute, also known as God, Brahman, Allah, the Infinite Creator, the One without a Second, and many more names. It is the seed vibration of all the archetypes, with never-ending potential consisting of a plethora of overtones and undertones. It is as though the Word, or Logos (from the Greek), was metamorphosized into the world through the vibration of light, the insertion of the *L* representing both the Logos and the Light. It shaped inert matter and produced a living, breathing universe.

Wor(L)d

The very word *universe* is a fascinating one to describe our vast environment. Its connotations are spiritual because *uni* means "one," and one meaning of *verse* is "turning." Literally, the universe is a turning toward the One. And as the word *verse* also refers to poetry and music, the meaning of "universe" can be expanded to "one song, one sounding out, or even one Word."

Verse = Turn

to the

Uni = One

Closely related to the sound of *verse* is the Latin word used in the Vulgate Bible for the Word or Logos:

Verbum = The Word, The Logos

From *verbum* is derived the English word *verb*. It refers to the active part of a sentence structure, just as the original Word's purpose is to reverberate and activate the inertness of matter through its pure desire and emotion. Here again a word reveals itself. Emotion is simply "the moving out from" in its basic meaning, a projection of something that has power and coloration. At the same time there is an ancestral precedent of the Word in the Sanskrit root *Vrt,* meaning "to come into being," transformed in the German to *Wort* (pronounced "vaurt").

There seems to be a connection between sound and words that begin with the *V* sound. *Verbum* itself, *V*ibration, and *V*oice, for example. Anyone who sounds a *V* on its own will feel how strong a sound it is—a great buzzing of the lips. Even the shape of the *V* as a series portrays a particular sound waveform, the sawtooth wave:

VVVVVVVV

This pattern is also a series of the letter *W,* the opening of *wave.* Closely connected with waves is "water," or in German, *Wasser,* in which the *W* is sounded as a *V.* The Biblical historian David Elkington has discovered that "the Word was with God and the Word was God" has ancient roots.[1] He traced the etymology of the word *God* back to the sound syllable *guth* from Old High Norse, which has the root meaning of "voice." At the center of the word *voice* lies our human essence, or individual Self, the *I.*

VOICE

This concept of the first primordial sound being likened to the projection of a voice into the void is nowhere better described than in Genesis, which describes the Supreme Being intoning a statement of what it desired and bringing it into existence:

And God said, "Let there be light and there was light." And God said, "Let the waters under the heaven be gathered together unto one place, and let the dry land appear." And it was so.

GENESIS 1:3 AND 1:9

In a similar vein there is the passage in Psalm 19:1–4 in the Old Testament:

The heavens declare the glory of God and the firmament shows his handiwork. Day unto day utters speech, and night unto night shows knowledge. There is no speech nor language where the voice is not heard. Their line is gone through all the earth, and their words to the end of the world. In them has he set a tabernacle for the sun.

The process was taken a step further when the first human, Adam, was given the role of naming the creatures:

And out of the ground the Lord God formed every beast of the field, and every fowl of the air; and brought them unto Adam to see what he would call them; and whatsoever Adam called every living creature, that was the name thereof.

GENESIS 19

The implication is that the sounding of the names, like archetypal vibratory formulae, actually fixes their physical manifestation. Such naming is mirrored in the Egyptian creation story in which Ra, the first god, arises out of the celestial waters sounding his own name, and thereafter creating other forms through utterances and visualizations.

Perhaps there is a link between the word *utter* in the context of giving birth to something, and the word *uterus,* the birth canal. Such manifestations through the archetypal voice are at the heart of St. John's Gospel:

> And the Word was made flesh and dwelt among us, and we beheld its glory, the glory as of the only begotten of the Father, full of grace and truth.
>
> JOHN 1:14

Here the voice of the Absolute, the Father in this case, intoned the name of his son, and that sound signature became the Son's flesh. The relationship between the word *son* (and even *sun*) and the French word for sound, *son,* is very apposite. Progenitors emanate vibrations that enliven inert matter and create flesh:

The Son (SOuNd or SoUNd) of God
The SOuNd of the Voice

These connections can also link to the word *person* from the Latin *personare,* "to sound through or resound." In effect, the Christ became the vibrational transmitter of the one voice. In terms of physics, they were in "sympathetic vibration." To quote the American physicist Dale Pond:

> The common connecting link between substance and energy is vibration. And the common vibratory phenomena that connects the vibration is sympathy. . . . In real human terms, we call sympathy or sympathetic association—LOVE. This is the Law that

binds individuals together. This is the Law that binds molecules together.[2]

As stated previously, the original Greek expression for the Word is the Logos. One of the definitions of the word *logos* is proportion and ratio, which has relevance to the phenomenon of sound as the progenitor of Creation. The nature of musical tones and their combinations, and the inner structure of matter when excited by sound are fundamentally based on proportions and ratios. The wisdom of the ancients has described a process of the unfoldment of Creation not as a "big bang," a term used by many physicists, but as something essentially musical, an intoning and chanting—in a phrase, "the enchantment of the universe." It could well be that the voice that chanted the Word preceded the later event known as the "big bang." In any case, the theories of certain cosmologists are beginning to be in accord with the Creation teachings of the ancient sages. Here is a newspaper report from *The Independent* (UK):

> Scientists have recorded the music of creation in an experiment using the astronomical equivalent of a time machine to go back to the origin of the universe. A telescope suspended from a high-altitude balloon circling the South Pole has detected harmonic "notes" which rung out like a bell in the first fractions of a second after the "Big Bang." Cosmologists believe that these minute ripples of sound became the "seeds" of matter, which eventually led to the formation of stars, galaxies and planets such as Earth.[3]

Mark Whittle, a cosmologist and professor at the University of Virginia, has produced these findings as part of his research in a field he calls Primordial Sound: Big Bang Acoustics:

It (the universe) would have begun in complete silence leading to a whisper, then a descending scream, building into a deep rasping roar, and ending with a deafening bass. The highest-pitch sounds ultimately spawn the first generation of stars, while the deep bass notes slowly dissolve to become the tapestry of galaxies. By looking at the ratio between the pitch of the notes, we can figure out what the actual chord is. For the two deepest notes in the cosmic chord, we find a slow change across the first million years from a major third to a minor third.* Stated more poetically, the Universe's symphony opens with a positive major chord, but as time passes, the mood shifts to a sadder one as the minor chord builds. [4]†

Carolin Crawford, professor of astronomy at Cambridge University, England, gave a similar vision of the universe when interviewed on BBC Radio:

---

*The major third is the distance between the note C and the note E going two white steps up to the right on the piano; the minor third is the distance between the note C and the second black key to the right, known as E flat on the piano.
†Here there is a curious connection to the symphonic tone poem, *Thus Spake Zarathrustra,* by German composer Richard Strauss. The opening measures of this work, representing the Superman, were chosen by Stanley Kubrick as the theme to underscore the beginning of Creation in his film *2001: A Space Odyssey.* Strauss very clearly moves from the major to the minor chord and vice versa several times, perhaps subconsciously producing the effect that Prof. Whittle describes.

When light and matter are no longer coupled, the light photons are free to stream towards us and this is the first point at which we can see what the universe was like. We see the minute fluctuations which have been caused by sound waves which went through the early universe. These fluctuations and densities go on to become the seeds and, as the universe grows, and expands, these seeds are the center around which galaxies and clusters of galaxies eventually form. So the sound waves have a crucial role in defining these structures.[5]

Ancient sages were able to perceive the Logos in its manifold manifestations, the echoes of which are still present in the universe. For example, Tibetan monks, by projecting their consciousness into space, have heard "the music of the spheres" and re-created these sounds in their gongs, bowls, bells, and trumpets, as well as in the depths of their voices.

In India, the original sound of Creation is recognized as the three-pronged seed *AUM*,* often shortened to *OM*. A complementary sound to *OM* is *HUM,* and when joined to the Sanskrit word for mind, *manas,* gives us the basis of who we are: HUMMANAS, or humanity. Similarly, in Sufisim one of the primary sounds expressing the nature of Allah, the Supreme Being, is *HUUU.* Mysteriously, the elision between *AUM* and the Sanskrit word *vac,* translated as "speech" but also associated with "transcendental sound," forms the English word:

---

*Metaphorically, there is visual symbolism of the *U* at the center of *AUM,* like a cup. "You" are filled with its holy spirit.

VAC(A)UUM

Although *vacuum* suggests emptiness and is a synonym for *void*, the deeper implication of its meaning is "vibrations beyond ordinary hearing." In fact, some quantum physicists have claimed that the so-called vacuum, in terms of subatomic particles, is a bustling world.[6]

The *AUM* or *OM*, as the earthly realization of the primordial utterance of the Absolute, has found its way into other languages. The Latin word *OMnes*, meaning "everything" and "all," yields such English words as *OMnipotence* and *OMnipresence*. It is represented in Greek by its opening and closing letters, *Alpha* and *OMega*. In German, the word *Raum*—*AUM* preceded by the fiery *R*—can be translated as "expanse," as in the space of the universe. In English it is related to "being," where the *U* in *AUM* slips away and *AM*, as in "I am," is the result. The I AM is our AIM, an anagram of I AM. Other *AM* sounds relevant to the Word are:

*A*to*M* = a basic unit of matter

*A*da*M* = the first human, as recorded in the Bible

*AM*en = a sacred sound originating in ancient Egypt and used in Christianity to signify assent

*A*t*M*an = the divine Self of Hinduism

*A*te*M* = breath (German) as in "breath of life" or *prana* (Sanskrit)

n*AM*e = to give something or someone a name to bring it into existence, as given in ancient Egyptian theology. *Name* is an anagram of *Amen*. In German the word is *Namen,* which is pronounced with the broad *AH* sound of *A*men.

The Mayans of Central America used the primordial seed sound *OL,* which includes the *O* aspect found in *OM*. The *O* connotes "awakened consciousness," and the *L,* "vibration."[7] In other words, vibration is the state of awakened consciousness. Other sounds related to the *AUM/OM* are:

*OM*en = a special sign from a higher source

N*UM*en = divine will or command of a deity (Latin)

N*AM*U = Self-power (Japanese)

N*AA*M = the beginning sound (Sikh)

N*AM* = the proclamation of an oracle (Hebrew)

So, from the vibration of the cosmic *AUM,* the ultimate reality projecting its sacred sound, a harmony of the universe, is made manifest. But how can we be aware of this phenomenon if we are fixed on the forms—the illusions, or *maya* as it is called in Indian philosophy—rather than the experience of the subtle pulses, the "unstruck sounds" (*anahata* in Sanskrit)? In Hindu cosmology the unfoldment of the universe is described in elemental terms. It begins with *akasha,* defined as both "space" and "sound." Its name in Western terms is the "ether," and it could also be the same as the "vacuum." The dictionary describes the ether as "a hypothetical substance supposed to occupy all space." It would seem to have an associative and verbal relationship to "et(H)ernity," the inserted *H* representing the "breath of life" and things "holy." The akasha contains and gives rise to the elements of air, fire, water, and earth. It suggests that the *AUM* is all the ripples of this akasha, endlessly interlocking and establishing an inner geometry of Creation. It could also be likened to a woven cosmic string instrument containing an infinite number of frequencies or rates of vibration.* The density of the akasha, as the *OM*nipresence of the Absolute, must be enormous, as according to the physics of sound, the denser the transmitter, the faster vibrations will travel. This principle helps us to understand the total interconnectedness of our universe.

What is the nature of sound and vibration? First, a distinction can be made between these two words. *Sound* is all that our physical ear and nervous system can perceive. *Vibration* is the complete gamut of frequencies, both audible and inaudible. Inaudible vibration can be sensed when our higher faculties are attuned. At the metaphysical level, vibration is the creative tension between the unmanifest and the manifest, and thus between action and repose, an interplay of opposites. On the one hand there is stillness and pure being without desire, and on the other, there is movement propelled by the desire to act. Before Creation began, the Absolute was in relative rest, just quietly throbbing. Then desire arose and it intoned the Word. This

---

*This concept resembles superstring theory, in which infinitesimal snips of subatomic particles vibrate in predetermined ways and interact with one another to create the properties of the particles of matter.

dichotomy established a tautness that became vibration, just as a violin string responds only when it is made taut—then the bow can set it in motion and the fingers can produce many different tones. Similarly, to be *taught* is to be receptive to, and resonate with knowledge received. The word *tone*, which is an anagram of *note*, its representation on paper, is derived from the Greek word *tonos*, meaning "tension."

The Creation of vibration begins with the initial force of pulsations. This can be observed when sound frequencies produced electronically become so low that a steady tone is replaced by pulsating blips. The pulses then send out various wave forms according to the means used to produce them—human voice, musical instruments, or forms of electronic technology. To perceive the pulses is to move toward the source of Creation, as is possible, for example, in the deepest mantra meditation.

Another major aspect of the sound phenomenon is its ability to shape matter and substance.[8] This is observable in living forms, including ourselves, where the relatively solid form is surrounded by a vibrating energy field. It holds the shape of whatever it is embracing. For example, when someone loses a limb, there can still be sensations where the limb used to be. The vibrational field is still wanting to hold the flesh together even though it has been removed.

Whether we recognize it or not we are riding on the crest of the Word with its infinite overtones and undertones. Every strand of this cosmic harp effect is within us, and that is why the universe is one colossal network wherein all is linked and therefore can lead us to the very source of our existence. The Word and the Wor(l)d in which we Whirl is infused with the Absolute. Should the Absolute discontinue to intone the Word, all the worlds would cease to exist. So we, too, must intone, emulate this sacred act and sustain our being.

2
The Nature of
the Chakras

We are a microcosm of Creation, an integral part of our universe. From the cellular aspect of the physical body all the way out to all the layers of the invisible energy field surrounding it, we should be vibrating in resonance with the natural harmony of Creation. That is the state of bliss described so well in Hindu philosophy, in which our minds are attuned to the one harmony and we have broken free of any self-imposed bonds from our previous lives and the present one.

From the spiritual perspective there are two essential parts of a human being—the silent divine witness and the soul. This witness who dispassionately sees and knows all is called the *atman* in Hinduism. It is our pure consciousness, our divine essence. The soul, or "causal body" (*antahkarana* in Sanskrit), whose center point lies between the heart and the throat according to yoga tradition, is the clearing house of all our tendencies and emotions and consists of all the invisible bodies described in various spiritual traditions (etheric, astral, emotional, intellectual, and so on). It is our psychology in all its aspects, and the objective is to effect its purification, or in vibrational terms, its re-tuning. These aspects are reflected in the different chakras that are components of the soul.

The Sanskrit word *chakra* is translated as "wheel," and derives from the Sanskrit root *car,* "to move." The chakras are spinning wheels of being (*bhava*) and of existence (*samsara*). They are psycho-energetic transformers composed of life energy (*prana*), interlinking the soul with our biology. They are part of our subtle body. Within the physical body they are positioned along the spine and also within the head.

They are seven in number, each aligned with one of the glands, and their levels of subtle energy become ever finer in the ascent from the base of the spine to the top of the head. This is illustrated in the yoga tradition, whereby the chakras, like the lotus blossom, are depicted as having an increasing number of "petals," from the lowest (root chakra) to the highest (crown chakra). The petals are the subsidiary vortices of energy within a given chakra, and they are powered by the breath—activated through inhalation and exhalation. Each chakra lotus has a certain number of petals, beginning with four for the root. The crown chakra has been assigned one thousand petals.

The chakras act as transformers that, functioning free of impurities, open us up to pure emotions and expanding states of consciousness. We can experience these processes through the complementary endocrine glands, as their hormones affect brain activity.

Harish Johari, a renowned writer on Eastern spirituality, gives this description:

Chakras can be thought of as wheels of the mind that dwell in the forest of desires. And desires, like wheels themselves, are great motivating forces. Each chakra is a stage-by-stage playground of desires, exhibiting its influence on the persons who are attached to the enjoyment of that particular chakra. Throughout life, one dwells in the forest and thinks and understands life's situations from the standpoint of the chakras in which one normally feels most comfortable. Each chakra becomes a stage for the psychodrama of electrochemical energy that expresses itself as behavior in human beings. As a result, there are specific behavioral characteristics associated with each chakra.[1]

From the Western perspective, Dr. Richard Gerber, in *Vibrational Medicine,* his definitive book on the topic, offers these concluding points about the relationship between the chakras and our emotions and physical body:

1. The major chakras are specialized energy transformers which take in subtle energy and distribute it to the major glands, nerve centers, and organs of the body.
2. The function of the chakras is related to various aspects of consciousness, especially the emotions, which affect the flow of energy through these centers. When the emotional body of the individual has a field disturbance related to emotional problems, that emotional disturbance becomes translated into an altered flow of energy through a particular chakra.
3. Each of the seven major chakras has a particular emotional and spiritual issue which affects its proper functioning. When an individual has significant unresolved emotional issues in

any one of these areas, chakra dysfunction may occur. Such dysfunction leads to the deprivation of nutritive subtle-energy flow to the bodily region and associated organs and glands supplied by that impaired chakra. If the chakra blockage is chronic, cellular imbalance and disease may eventually occur.

4. Altered subtle energetic flow through the various chakras is one mechanism by which chronic stress can negatively affect the physical body.[2]

Physical Disorders Related to the Chakras

The imbalance of a particular chakra can sometimes be brought to our attention by recurring and/or persistent physical disturbances in the body.

Root: hemorrhoids, constipation, sciatica, spine/sacrum disorders

Sacral: impotence, frigidity, cystitis, disorders of the uterus, bladder, or kidneys

Solar plexus: digestive disorders, diabetes, ulcers, hypoglycemia

Heart: disorders of the heart and lungs, disorders of the immune system, high blood pressure, asthma

Throat: sore throat, laryngitis, tonsillitis, possible loss of hearing

Brow: sight loss, headaches, dyslexia

Crown: beyond the physical

There is no automatic process whereby the chakras can simply convert negative emotions into positive. What exists in the soul can cause abnormalities in the flow of energy through a chakra. If their rate of spin is out of balance or even moving in the wrong direction, they are placing palpable stress on the physiological system as the connecting element between the subtle energy world and the physical body. To restore these centers to their purest state through sound is to modify their frequencies so that the wheels are whirling at their proper rate. When there is a blockage in a chakra it means negative emotions associated with that particular center have not dissipated, and have disturbed that chakra's frequencies. As the mis-tunings are corrected, our state of consciousness expands and there is increasing freedom from the dominance of the impediments held in the chakra.

The main issues of the seven principal chakras are:

Root (the earth element): Rootedness and groundedness in the earth plane so as to feel a natural security in our surroundings. A center that is concerned with survival and generates a primary fear when our physical life is threatened. Such fear can go too far and turn into paranoia or, in an underactive condition, cause the loss of the basic will to survive. It concerns our physical identity, embodiment, and self-acceptance.

Sacral chakra (the water element): Also known as the spleen chakra, it is linked with our reproductive organs and is the center for the subtle energy of our sexuality and sensual emotions in general. It is also a flowing portal for our creativity when the sexual energy becomes transmuted into a higher form. It is our emotional identity, a source of vitality and the center for self-gratification.

Solar plexus chakra (the fire element): This is a center that concerns our will, authority, courage, assertiveness, and personal power. In its negative phase it expresses itself as anger, domination, and aggression, or their opposites—cowardice, fear, and submissiveness.

Heart chakra (the air element): The mediating chakra between the lower and higher ones, it is the focal point of our love and compassion for both others and ourselves, and engenders patience. Here is the source of commitment and conscience, and also our experience of pure grief. Linked to the thymus gland, its positive activation will stimulate this gland and thus support the all-important immune system.

Throat chakra (the ether element): Essentially this is the center for communication and expression, and because of its connection to the sense of hearing, our ability to listen to others without judgment.

Brow chakra: Often referred to as the "third eye," this is the seat of our intuition and higher awareness, and enables us to receive insights into the events of our lives. Here is our psychic perception, clairvoyance, and introspection, the place in which perceiving the world as duality begins to dissolve.

Crown chakra: This is the portal to our highest states of consciousness and the full flowering of our spirituality. It is the place where the great Self rules supreme, there is a transcendence of opposites, and we live in oneness.

As the chakras are related to psychological, emotional, and spiritual states, we can conclude that they are an extension of our soul. The soul is the seedbed, so to speak, of all the possible traits that have been imprinted into us from previous lives. It becomes a question of which ones we manifest in this lifetime. To a large extent, this imprint is what is revealed through an astrological birth chart. Furthermore, it contains all the cumulative experiences of the present life. Any healing work directed to the chakras, the mediators between the invisible and visible bodies, is consequently the purification of our soul life, a clearly spiritual process.

Dr. Gerber presents this overall picture of the chakra hierarchy:

The first three centers (root, sacral, and solar plexus chakras) form a lower triad of physiologic and grounding functions. The uppermost three centers (throat, brow, and crown chakras) form the higher spiritual triad. . . . The heart chakra is the bridge between the lower and the higher triads. It is only through the manifesting of one's higher love nature that one can unite the higher and lower energies. The ultimate expression and the unfoldment of the heart chakra is unconditional love and the active demonstration of the Christ consciousness.[3]

3

The Psychology of the Chakras as Related to Vowels and Consonants

We take language for granted; it develops in us and becomes our fundamental means of communication. At an early age we learn the alphabet and how the letters are sounded in their various combinations. We listen and learn how to string together vowels and consonants and create words without ever giving it another thought. The learning of a language is rarely ritualized in such a way that each vowel and consonant sound is explored as a world unto itself, a special cell within the larger body having its own individual feeling. Visionary thinker Rudolf Steiner was among the few to focus on this. Within the curriculum he created known as Waldorf education, he developed sound and movement rituals for learning the alphabet, which he called Eurhythmy. The sounds are invested with purpose and emotion and allow students to access the archetypal world of forms.

It is assumed that all the nonsense sounds young children project are their way of developing their native tongue. However, it is quite possible they are blissfully enjoying the vocal sounds for their own sake. They have recently come into material being from the world of spirit and are producing, in effect, an archetypal sound world. But even as adults we enjoy the play of vowel and consonant sounds. In states of heightened emotion we produce all manner of compact sound expressions, including laughter, groaning, wailing, sighing, and humming. Some of us are attracted to puns, the play of words, as are newspapers in their headlines. At the highest level of language as pure sound, we have poets and lyricists who enhance our emotions through rhyming, alliteration, and onomatopoeia.

There are certain languages in which the alphabet is invested with special meanings and qualities. Regarding the letters of the Hebrew alphabet, Edward Hoffman, author of *The Hebrew Alphabet,* writes:

> The Hebrew alphabet bears a host of hidden significances. In traditional Jewish thought, each letter—its name, pictorial form, numerical equivalent, and respective position in the alphabet—is ordained by God.[1]

He refers to the mystic Abraham ben Samuel Abulafia (ca. 1240–1292):

> Abulafia taught in a practical way that the Hebrew letters are a key pathway—in fact, the means for "the soul to actualize its

potential with much greater ease" than with any other method. He emphasized that through proper understanding and practice, any person can use the Hebrew language as a means to arouse tremendous intuitive capabilities. "Look at these holy letters with truth and belief," he advised, "it will awaken the heart to thoughts of godly and prophetic images."[2]

Similarly, the Sanskrit language of India is invested with great significance, as we are told by the living musician, sound therapist, and mystic, Sri Shyamji Bhatnagar:

> According to the spiritual tradition of ancient India, basic truths of the universe reverberate subtly, eternally, and everywhere. It is said that in the current epoch, before recorded history, they were first heard by unusually gifted intuitives. The language in which these truths were received was Sanskrit. . . . Tradition teaches that the sounds of Sanskrit were used to create the universe and all objects within it. The fifty-two sounds of the Sanskrit alphabet encompass most of the sounds found in the major languages of the world since ancient times. The creative potential of Sanskrit is at the root of the mysterious power of mantra . . . the tradition provides a sophisticated Sanskrit vocabulary with which to describe the fundamental laws of the universe and the spiritual nature of human beings.[3]

Comparing the spoken word with the sung word, it is obvious that our voices are designed for more than communication of ideas, thoughts, feelings, commands, and so on. A transformation of language takes place when the vowels and consonants are set to music. While there is still communication through the text, there are now new aspects: the changing of the pitch and timbre of the voice, the possible "vibrato," changing rhythms, and above all, the prolongation of individual vowel sounds on more than one tone.

When singing is taken one step further and totally distilled into small packets of sound it becomes toning, a term often used in the sound therapy field. These packets can be in the form of vowels, consonants, or single syllables. Through toning these are transformed into pure sound phenomena that penetrate and sympathetically resonate our energy centers. The sounds become sacralized, and thus are healing. Vocal sounds, whatever their spiritual source, are not automatically sacred. It is we who transform them by our intention and the ways we create and use them. An interesting example of ordinary vocal sound and sacralized sound is found in Sufism, which has many names for the Absolute. One of them is *HUUU*. It is identical to the word *WHO*. No one takes the latter to be a sacred sound. So what is the difference between the two? It is the way the Sufis intone and prolong the sound within their religious ceremonies with the greatest depth of feeling for the Godhead. They have made the sound transcendental. It also gives an answer to the fundamental philosophical question, "*WHO* am I?" By reversing the question we have the answer: "I am *HUUU*." So the power of the mind to elevate sound to the spiritual level cannot be underestimated. Clearly, it is our intention, pure emotion, and desire that make the difference.

As all is in a state of vibration, whether audible or not, each with its own frequency, it is natural to use the principle of resonance as a mode of healing; that is, to produce sympathetic vibrations that mirror what is to be healed. The object is to get the chakras to recognize their sonic nature by sending out those frequencies to which they will attune. This process is a kind of vocal homeopathy based on the idea that like cures like. The most effective immediate resonator is attested to by the spiritual traditions that use mantras and chanting as an aid to enlightenment.

The vowels are the primary sounds, as they provide a richness of harmonics or overtones* that render the voice as an organic healing instrument. Research has shown that there is no Eastern tradition of correlating vowels with chakras. Rather, the choice of which vowels correspond to what chakras has developed from an intuitive general consensus among Western sound therapists. The way it took root in Western circles is a mystery, but there is a fair degree of agreement among practitioners. For example, surveying seven major practitioners, all agreed that *AH* and *EE* are linked to the heart and crown, respectively.

---

*Overtones, also known as harmonics, are the subtle higher frequencies embedded in a heard fundamental tone. These upper vibrations are like the aura of the composite tone, giving musical tones their unique color and richness. They are naturally produced on the vowels, and various vocal techniques can make them individually audible. It could be hypothesized that the aura spectrum of overtones increases the ability of the tones to do healing work.

Practitioners' Choices of Vowels for
Toning with the Chakras

The survey below of seven major practitioners (not including this author), all of whom have written books on sound healing, shows their preferences for chakra/vowel correspondences.

Root	4 *UH*	3 *OO*	
Sacral	4 *OO*	2 *OH* I *UH*	
Solar plexus	4 *OH*	3 *AW*	
Heart	7 *AH*		
Throat	4 *EH*	2 *AY*	I *EYE*
Brow	5 *EE*	I *AY*	I *IH*
Crown	7 *EE*		

The vowels I recommend for re-tuning the chakras are a result of both my intuition and experience and have some correspondences with other sound therapists. In three instances—the solar plexus, the throat, and the brow—two vowels are given that are close in sound, allowing individuals to use their intuition to decide which they prefer. It is important to understand that individuality plays its part in sound healing, and these slight differences can be felt by those who practice toning. One of the leading authorities in the therapeutic use of sound, Don Campbell, expressed this succinctly: "What we have to accept is that no one form of sound therapy works for everybody."[4]

VOWELS FOR TONING

Chakra	Vowel
Root	*UH* as in *hug*
Sacral	*O* as in *food*
Solar Plexus	*OH* as in *know* and *AW* as in *raw*
Heart	*AH* as in *father*
Throat	*AY* as in *say* and *EH* as in *head*
Brow	*I* as in *eye* and *IH* as in *hit*
Crown	*EE* as in see

Five of the seven consonants I have chosen to correlate to the first five energy centers, namely *L, V, R, Y,* and *H* are drawn from the Tantra tradition of *bijas,* or seed syllables. These seeds, central to the Tantra tradition, are monosyllabic and not invested with meaning. They are brief seed formulae used repetitively to awaken the potential energies found in the chakras. They consist of an opening consonant, followed by a consistent vowel and a closing humming *M.*

SEED SOUNDS FROM TANTRA

Chakra	Seed Sound
Root	*LAM*
Sacral	*VAM*
Solar Plexus	*RAM*
Heart	*YAM*
Throat	*HAM*
Brow	*OM*
Crown	Silence

These threefold seed syllables are discontinued at the brow and crown chakras. Instead, *OM* is used for the brow, while the crown chakra is considered to be beyond audible sound.

In my adapted version of the seed syllables presented below, the opening consonants of the Tantra seed syllables are combined with the Western vowel system, with a closing *M* sound. For example, the adapted seed syllable for the root chakra is *L* + *UH* + *M* to form *LUHM* and for the solar plexus chakra *R* + *AW* + *M* to form *RAWM*. In addition, the opening consonants *S* and *K* have been intuitively selected for the brow and crown chakras, respectively.* This offers more choices in the practice of toning the chakras. The humming *M,* an important part of the seed syllables, also has a role to play among the consonants as an all-embracing sound for all the chakras.

ADAPTED SEED SYLLABLES

Chakra	Seed Sound
Root	LUHM
Sacral	VOOM
Solar Plexus	RAWM
Heart	YAHM
Throat	HAYM
Brow	SIM
Crown	KEEM

---

*Some offshoots of the Tantra tradition assign the syllable *KSHAM* to the brow and reserve *OM* for the crown. I decided intuitively to use *S* and *K* for the brow and crown, respectively, before discovering that the *KSHAM* opens with these two consonants.

Extracting the consonants from the seed syllables is similar to the process whereby vitamins and minerals are taken from foods and prepared as concentrated supplements. If we take the vowels and consonants to be nourishment for the soul, then the vowels become the vitamins, the consonants the minerals.

It is the hypothesis of this book that the vowels of our Western toning tradition and the consonants derived from Tantra are sounds that lie in the collective unconscious mind. These sounds are to be found at the beginning of many words, and in the case of vowels, in a significant position in a word relating directly to the chakra's psychology—both positive and negative characteristics—and corresponding element and sense. Thus, the primary feature of the succeeding descriptions of the chakras is the prominent use of such words. The purpose is to awaken deeper levels of our psychology so that we experience each consonant and vowel as a feeling presence embedded in a word. It suggests that the sounds of language are archetypal, that the sounds are not entirely arbitrary but arise out of the collective unconscious. The associative words are drawn almost exclusively from the English language with occasional references to German, Latin, Greek, Sanskrit, and Hebrew. Our concern is with the sounds and not the actual letters. So hard *C* and *K*, soft *C* and *S* (in English), *J* and *Y* (in German), and *W* and *V* (in German) are linked. In appendix V there are also some speculative ideas about the shapes of the letters and their possible connection to the psychology of the chakras.

Such an approach of language associations does invite criticism because, obviously, not all words containing a particular vowel or consonant sound relate to the corresponding chakra. For example, why should the word *moot,* containing the vowel *OO* as in *food,* relate to the corresponding sacral chakra? There is no answer to this charge other than that one cannot expect all the *OO* words to conform. The other criticism questions why this association is largely based on the English language. English is a very rich language built from many sources, and has become the principal *lingua franca* of the world. Why this has occurred goes beyond the dominance of the world by first Great Britain and then the United States. The seeding of a language has a deeper meaning than any rational explanation. Only through reading expositions about the element, sense, flowering, and inhibiting of the chakras can the reader possibly accept that there is something in the collective unconscious reflected in the sounds of our language that connect with the psychology of the chakras.

4
The Root Chakra

Sanskrit name:	*Muladhara* (foundation and support)
Location:	Base of the spine
Endocrine gland:	Adrenals
Element:	Earth
Sense:	Smell
Natural characteristics:	Security, stability, rootedness survival, self-preservation, physical identity, hunger
Vowel:	*UH* as in *hUHg*
Consonant:	*L*
Tantra seed syllable:	*LAM*
Adapted seed syllable:	*LUHM*

The root chakra is located at the base of the spine where there is a hub of nerves, most notably the sciatic nerve that extends down the *L*egs and *L*oins to the feet. Thus, this chakra connects us with the earth, the *L*and itself, and the richness of its *L*oam. The earth, when saturated with water, becomes m*UH*d, and when deprived of it turns to d*UH*st. The fertile land mixed with d*UH*ng produces an unmistakable sm*ELL* sensed by the *OL*factory nerves, the sense associated with this chakra.

Physically, the *L*ower region of the body has aspects whose names, including colloquial ones, contain the *L* consonant and/or the *UH* vowel. Part of the body's lower region is the *LUH*mbar, whose opening syllable is identical to the adapted seed syllable. Others are: f*UH*ndament, b*UH*ttocks, b*UH*m, r*UH*mp, g*UH*t, *L*abia, v*UL*va, and *Lingam* (Sanskrit for phallus).*

At the base of the spine lies the dw*ELL*ing place of the k*UH*ndalini, the fundamental spiritual energy. This is the pure motive force of *LUH*ve, the elixir of *L*ife and the producer of *L*ight† that leads to *L*iberation of the true s*EL*f. Its path is to rise through the chakras like blissful bubbles of *L*aughter (*L*evity), and will gradually do so if we can purify the channels. The very syllable *EL* is the Hebrew for "holy one," found similarly in the Babylonian and Sumerian languages meaning "the radiant one." It appears in the Hebrew plural in the Book of Genesis as *EL*ohim. To the Muslim it is becoming one with A*LL*lah (the A*LL*-embracing one), and to the Christian it

---

*In chapter 2 there is a listing of physical disorders generally associated with each of the chakras.
†Other words of significance regarding *L*ight are: *L*uminosity, i*LL*umination, *L*ucidity, *L*amp, *L*antern, *L*uster, g*L*eam and g*L*ow.

is the ecstasy of the a*LL*e*L*uia. At the root chakra resides the p*UL*sation of the Word or *L*ogos. We have to surrender, an a*LL*owing and *L*etting go, to its *EL*emental *AL*chemy. This is true security, just as a child feels secure as it is h*UH*gged by its m*UH*ther or listens to a *LULL*aby. In religious terms our s*UH*pport is in placing tr*UH*st in and feeling the s*UH*pport of the *L*ord or Absolute.

To be grounded in this world is to not be v*UL*nerable, *L*ost, *L*ocked, *AL*ien, and *AL*one within yourself. This sense of separation, n*ULL*ifying yourself from the real you, becomes a heavy *L*oad and *L*abor, as in "to be *LUH*mbered with." One feels *L*ow, *L*istless, *L*ethargic, *L*azy, d*UHLL*, *L*ame, *L*imited, and *L*acking in energy. This is the earthly h*ELL* where, due to a false sense of security, people are st*UH*ck in the *L*etter of the *L*aw rather than listening to their inner voice. It is a self-inflicted p*UH*nishment.

At the physical level our natural sense of security is to satisfy our h*UH*nger in order to survive. But there are other hungers that attempt to a*LL*eviate our separation. When *LUH*ve has been distorted by the impure ego, and is replaced only by the physical act of sex, then it turns into its polar opposite—*LUH*st. There are a number of *L* and *UH* words which describe or allude to the debasement of physical love: *L*echery, *L*asciviousness, *L*ewd, *L*urid, *L*eer, i*LL*icit, *LUH*re, a*LL*ure, sed*UH*ction, s*UL*try, and, last but not least, the vulgar word f*UH***.

5
The Sacral Chakra

Sanskrit name:	*Svadhishthana* (one's dwelling place)
Location:	Upper sacrum below the navel
Endocrine glands:	Gonads, ovaries
Element:	Water
Sense:	Taste
Natural characteristics:	Procreation, sexuality, creativity, sensuality, self-gratification, desire, and fantasy
Vowel:	*OO* as in *fOOd*
Consonant:	*V*
Tantra seed syllable:	*VAM*
Adapted seed syllable:	*VOOM*

The sacral chakra (sometimes referred to as the spleen chakra) is immersed in the fl*OO*id element of Water. Although in English this letter is usually called a double *U*, it is written as a double *V*. To write a series of *V* letters is to draw a picture of a sawtooth *W*ave in physics.

VVVVVVVVVV

Not only are there the associated words of *W*ater and *W*ave, but there are also *W*et, *W*ash, *W*eep, and *W*ell. Moreover, the German word for water, *Wasser,* is pronounced "*V*asser," indicating decisively that this element has a strong link to the *V*ibration of *V*. Liquids can be measured for their *V*iscosity.* The *OO* vowel has its strong watery connections in such words as *OO*ze, s*OO*the, del*OO*ge, sol*OO*tion, dil*OO*tion, l*OO*brication, d*OO*ce, dr*OO*l, and p*OO*l.†

The sacral chakra is associated with the sense of taste, and in f*OO*d we have the basic substance that we taste. There are two further *V* words that connect to food and therefore, to taste—*V*iands and *V*ictuals.

The sacral chakra is highly feminine in nature, represented by the m*OO*n and situated alongside the *W*oman's *W*atery *WOO*mb. The *V* consonant marks out physical aspects of a woman in such words as *V*agina, *V*ul*V*a, o*V*aries, y*OO*terus, *V*estal *V*irgin, and *V*enus-like. Women are also labelled negatively as *V*ixens and *V*iragos.

Within the sacral chakra are two components of our nature:

---

*The definition of viscosity is "the property of a liquid, gas, or semifluid that enables it to offer resistance to flow.

†Another word relevant to water that contains the *OO* is flood, although the word does not use the requisite vowel sound.

creativity at different levels and sexuality in the procreative sense. When the creativity is in full flow, it can be *V*isceral and expresses our *V*itality and enth*OO*siasm, the *V*im* and *V*igor of that energy that projects wh*OO* we are. Just as the natural *V*ernal world bl*OO*ms and is fr*OO*tful, so we, when in full flight, simply d*OO*, prod*OO*ce, ind*OO*ce, and make n*OO*, tuning into our *V*oice† of ingen*OO*ity. This is the freedom of y*OO*, a wise f*OO*l brimming with the j*OO*ces of playfulness and lighthearted humor.

Within the creative act of sex is variously expressed sensuality, playfulness, chastity, repression, and wantonness. In traditional courtships, men w*OO* the opposite sex while the women c*OO* in response. Men† can emphasize their *V*irility while women might play up their *V*oluptuousness. On the other hand, there is the *V*irtuous *V*irgin who holds to her *V*ows. At the same time, repressed sexuality turns people into pr*OO*des who might secretly have pr*OO*rient interests.

All excessive desires are characterized by *V*oracity and a*V*idity. So, for example, those who indulge in physical sex can be caught in a web of *V*ice, possibly subjecting themselves to *V*enereal diseases. The blockage of the sexual energy of this chakra produces the desire to lash out at others, playing the role of the *V*illain as they accost their *V*ictims. It can manifest as *V*iolence, *V*iciousness, *V*ehemence, *V*indictiveness, *V*engeance, *V*endettas, *V*iolation, *V*ileness, and *V*enom.

---

*The word *Vim* is unique in that expresses the essence of the chakra and is also very close to the Tantra seed syllable of *VAM*.

†The voice is an instrument of creativity and, in the case of all of Creation, the instrument of the Absolute that sounded the Word or Logos.

†One slang word for man is *dOOde*.

6

The Solar Plexus Chakra

Sanskrit Name:	*Manipura* (city of jewels)
Location:	Between the navel and the bottom of the sternum
Endocrine gland:	Pancreas
Element:	Fire
Sense:	Sight*
Natural Characteristics:	Willpower, courage, self-esteem, self-assertion, autonomy, authority, resolution, dominion
Vowels:	*OH* as in *rOHw* and *AW* as in *rAW*
Consonant:	*R*
Tantra seed syllable:	*RAM*
Adapted seed syllable:	*RAWM*

---

*The ancient Egyptian word *ra* means "light," which is fundamental to being able to see.

In the sonic theology of India, the vibration for the fi*R*e element is given as *R*, reflected in the Tantra seed syllable *RAM* for the s*OH*lar plexus chakra. This correspondence between *R* and fi*R*e lies within the subconscious mind. When we hug ourselves and blurt out the sound of *BRRRR* because we are so cold, we are hoping that this vibration of the *R* will somehow give us the wa*R*mth we want. In the English language there are several words that refer to the nature of fi*R*e and have a pronounced *R* sound: bu*R*n, wa*R*m, infe*R*no, f*R*iction, *R*age, *R*ay, *ROH*ar, and *ROH*ast. The last two words also contain the complementary vowel of *OH*, as do these fire-related words: sm*OH*ke, sm*OH*lder, and gl*OH*w.

To work with the s*OH*lar plexus chakra is to use its qualities of pow*ER* and cou*R*age toward spiritual advancement. When we trust that the Absolute is the source of that pow*ER* for right action, we can then be he*ROH*ic, b*R*ave, *ROH*bust, b*OH*ld, *AW*dacious, and int*R*epid, and take *R*isks. We take hold of a situation and, like a s*OH*ldier with the *RAW* emotion of cou*R*age, shouting *HOH*, defend our d*OH*minion and assert our *AW*thority.

We are able to maintain our truth and say "N*OH*" with discrimination and without losing our integrity. In this chakra we can see in our mind's eye (the *R*etina)* our *ROH*le and g*OH*als, and *R*ecognize when we fall short of the mark and c*OH*pe with our *ER*rors. Through *R*eason and sensible c*AW*tion we sense our coherent p*UR*pose and then are required to hold our n*ER*ve, overcome our psychological f*OH*es, and be *R*esolute, fi*RM*, ea*R*nest, self-*R*eliant, s*OH*ber, and, above all, *OH*bedient to that

---

*The retina is connected with sight, which is the sense linked to the solar plexus chakra.

gut feeling that kn*OH*ws. In a word, we g*OH* forward with our *R*ites* of passage and true c*AW*ses, and bring a natural *OH*rder to our lives. Through the fi*R*e in the belly (abd*OH*men, p*AW*nch), *R*ubbish is incinerated and the chakra is purified.

When out of balance, the fi*R*e element can be either too weak or too strong. In its weakened condition it is held in check by fea*R*, wo*RR*y, c*OH*wardice, l*OH*neliness, *AW*kwardness, and general w*OH*e, just as we are by the l*AW*. It gives us an *AW*ful, gn*AW*ing feeling of being wr*AW*ght with all the *AW*ghts and *R*igid *R*egimens of life. The sense of duty without love creates a t*AW*tness and c*OH*ldness that could e*R*upt in gr*OH*aning, m*OH*aning, or b*AW*ling. Instead of being free to live out our convictions, we are c*AW*ght and h*AW*nted by illusory f*AW*lts and fl*AW*s, and hemmed in by h*AW*ghtiness.

On the other hand, self-assertion becomes quite out of control as the fi*R*e within us *R*ages with Ang*ER*, fu*R*y, *AR*gumentiveness, *R*ants, *R*etorts, *R*udeness, and *R*ambunctiousness. We turn into *R*ebellious, *R*ough, *R*evengeful, and *R*uinous persons whose destructive nature can manifest as *R*ampages, *R*iots, *R*apes, w*R*eckages *R*uptures, *R*outs, *R*avages, *R*umpuses, *R*ansackings, and *R*abble *R*ousing. This c*AW*stic fi*R*e *R*uns amok, *R*ushes about, *R*idicules, *R*ends, *R*ips, initiates *R*ows, stirs up a *R*acket, and sees *R*ed. These are the *R*ogues of the world who *R*ock society, and in the extreme, are bearers of h*OR*R*o*R and te*R*R*o*R.

---

*The words *rite* and *ritual* derive from the Sanskrit word *rita,* which means "universal order."

7

The Heart Chakra

Sanskrit name:	*Anahata**
Location:	Center of chest on sternum
Endocrine gland:	Thymus†
Element:	Air‡
Sense:	Touch
Natural Characteristics:	Unconditional love, compassion, devotion, forgiveness
Vowel:	*AH* as in *fAHther*
Consonant:	*Y* as in *Yearn*
Tantra seed syllable:	*YAM*
Adapted seed syllable:	*YAHM*

---

*Anahata means "unstruck" in relation to sound. It is vibration beyond that of anything physical that would involve two objects creating the sound. It is a supersensual, cosmic vibration known in Sanskrit as *shabda brahman*.

†At the center of the word *thymus* lies the heart consonant *Y,* and its first syllable addresses the spiritual heart, as in "hallowed be Thy name." Here *name* is also Thy sound and Thymus(ic).

‡The principal ingredient of air is oxygen, and situated in the middle of the word lies the heart consonant *Y.*

All the great religions of the world have at their center the fundamental precept that we have to love one another and "do unto others as we would have them do unto us." The chakra that transmits our love is the heart, elevating the energies arising in the three lower chakras and serving as the conduit to the upper three chakras.

It is significant that the revered ones of the world's religions have names that contain the broad *AH* vowel. The most prominent and perhaps most powerful of these is *AHLLAH,* the supreme name among many for God in Islam. It might be overlooked that the very word *God* is sounded as G*AH*d. In Judaism there is *YAH*weh and *YAH*ehov*AH,* in Hinduism Br*AH*hm*AH* and the primary gods Krishn*AH* and Shiv*AH,* in Buddhism Budd*HAH,* in T*AH*oism the teaching of the T*AH*o, and in Aramaic Coptic Christianity, *AH*woon*AH* and the famous Egyptian god *AH*tem-R*AH.* The Sanskrit words *AH*nahata (cosmic sound), *AH*nanda (bliss), and *AH*tman (divine essence) begin with the heart-centered *AH.* In Christianity, Jesus's name is linked to the *Y* consonant in the Aramaic form of *Y*eshua and in its Germanic form of *Jesu (Yayzoo).* And in Genesis we have the first human in his perfection, *AH*dam.

The centrality of the heart, both spiritually and physically, is symbolized within the many alphabets that begin with the letter *A.* Two prime examples are the Greek *AHL*pha and the Hebraic *AHL*eph, each adjoined with the root chakra *L.*

In English the association between the *Y* consonant and the heart comes foremost in the pronoun *You.* In other words, to be truly *You* means that, through the heart, individuals (nondivided beings) connect with each other (*Y*ounity) in love (*AH*mo in Latin, *AH*gape in Greek, and *AH*mour in French), revealed by acts of compassion, such as offering *AH*lms and forgiveness. In these acts we

*Y*ield ourselves to others. Thus, the greatest *You* (or *Ye*) becomes the Supreme Being. This is significant in certain Christian traditions that, in modern times, have changed the language referring to God from *Thee* and *Thine* to *You* and *Your,* more descriptive of the Holy One. In addition to the *Y* of the heart, the flow of God's creative juices is in the *OO*.

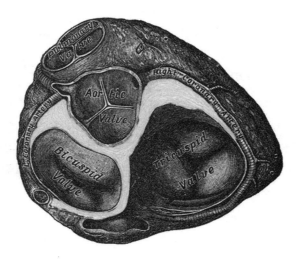

Within the physical heart can be seen the outline
of the letter Y. Its shape embraces and delineates
the bicuspid, aortic, and tricuspid valves.

The heart is a place of *AH*ffirmation, *Ah*ccord, and *Ah*greement, where we *AH*ssent to the glory of life itself. This *AH*ssent is very well expressed in the Christian words *AH*men and *AH*lleluia. In German the affirmative is even more heart-centered as *JAH.** So

---

*In German the letter *J* is sounded as an English *Y*. In *Ja,* the heart vowel and consonant are joined together. This also applies to the German word *Juwel* mentioned in this chapter.

when individuals say "*Yes*" to whatever is before them or asked of them, they are speaking from the heart and *AH*llowing their essence to freely flow. The heart center becomes as a h*AH*rp on which we strum the strings and accompany our Ps*AH*lms. This jubilation* (German: *der Jubel*†) is expressed in all sorts of ways, including l*AH*ghter and d*AH*ncing.‡

The very word *heart* (h*AH*rt) has, at its center, the *AH* vowel preceded by the spiritual breath of *H*. Our hearts, full of *AH*ffection and *AH*doration, Yearn (also Yen) to know the true Self (Sanskrit: *AH*tman) and that of others. We long for the rapture, bliss (Sanskrit: *AH*nanda) and then union (Yoke, Yoga) with this Self, and a return to the innocence of our Youth when we were literally "*Young* at heart." Metaphorically speaking, we surrender ourselves to a very loving f*AH*ther (*pAHter* in Latin) and *mAHter* (Latin for *mother*).

Through the *AH*rdour for union with the true Self, a b*AH*lm is secreted from the heart, a b*AH*nd develops between our soul and spirit, and we come to *AH*tonement ("at oneness"). The w*AH*rmth and f*AH*ndness of the heart, like a precious jewel (German: *Juwel*), is an open h*AH*rth bestowing c*AH*lmness and h*AH*rmony.

It is the h*AH*rt that is h*AH*rdened like a r*AH*ck, tied up in

---

*An exclamatory word of jubilation and joy beginning with the heart *Y* is *Yay,* meaning *hurray.*

†Other significant words of the heart in German, in which the *J* is sounded as *Y* are: *jammer* (lamentation), *janken* (to hanker after), *jauchzen* (to rejoice), *Joch* (yoke), and *jung* (young).

‡In British English as opposed to American English, the words *laughter* and *dancing* are often pronounced with the broad *AH* (long vowel).

kn*AH*ts that must be softened and released. The d*AH*rkness of this condition turns into *A*nimosity, *A*ntipathy, *A*pathy, *A*nguish and *A*nxiety.* The condition inflicts h*AH*rm and h*AH*rshness on others as well as the Self. The l*AH*menting, s*AH*mber, and s*AH*bbing heart must be *AH*ssuaged and *Y*ield to the natural joy of its energy center. Rather than experiencing *AH*loneness, we re-tune this chakra and know everything to be *AH*ll-one. It asks that we be touched and create a sympathetic *A*tmosphere (*A*ir) of love, compassion, and peace (Latin: *pAHx*).

---

*These are significant words beginning with a variant on the *AH* sound. This variant appears in words very compatible with the heart, including h*A*ppiness, comp*A*ssion, and *A*tmosphere.

8
The Throat Chakra

Sanskrit name:	*Vishuddha* (purity)
Location:	Between larynx and collarbone on the neck
Endocrine gland:	Thyroid
Sense:	Hearing
Element:	Akasha (ethereal space and sound)
Natural Characteristics:	Communication, self-expression, purification
Vowels:	*AY* as in *sAY* and *EH* as in *hEHd*
Consonant:	*H*
Tantra seed syllable:	*HAM*
Adapted seed syllable:	*HAYM*

The breath sound of *H* is a natural and pure sound. Many primary words beginning with *H* relate to positive states of being as applied to *H*umanity: *H*ealing, *H*oliness, (w)*H*oleness, *H*appiness, *H*umility, *H*armony, *H*umour,* *H*ome, *H*ope, and *H*allowness. When the breath is flowing freely through the throat chakra, its expression reflects such qualities. The *H* sound gives us the psychological polarity of *H*eaven and *H*ell, and also describes the three *H*uman essentials of *H*ead, *H*and, and *H*eart. And the German word for *throat* is *H*als. The joy of laughter is on the breath in its various expressions: *H*uh, *H*oh, *H*ah, *H*eh, and *H*ee. If the eyes are the windows of the soul, then the throat is the doorway of same, and we know how much of a person's psychology can be detected through the voice.

Communication involves both speaking and listening, so it is right that this chakra connects with the sense of *H*earing.† We *H*arken to experience the *Akasha* of ethereal sound and sp*AY*ce as it reverberates its silent *H*allelujah. An *AY*m is to pr*AY* for *H*ealing and, in gratefulness, pr*AY*se and procl*AY*m the Holy One's n*AY*me. In effect, we ask for *H*elp, the greatest *H* word of communication, perhaps through the intermediaries of *A*Yngels (literally, messengers).

In the mundane world of communication we s*AY* (or in past tense, s*EH*d) these words as greetings: *Hello, Hey, Hi, Ho,* and even *H*ail. "*H*ow are you?" is also representative. To release our joy we excl*AY*m "*H*urrah" and "*H*ooray." In the animal kingdom there are the communicative sounds of the b*AY*ing dog and the n*AY*ghing horse.

---

*The word *Humour* (British spelling of *humor*) has been cleverly interpreted as the "love of God." It is the joining together of one of the Sufi names for God, *HU,* with the French word for love—*amour.*

†In Latin the word *oboedio* means "to listen to," and from it is derived the English word ob*AY*. It has the spiritual connotation of listening to the inner voice, or conscience.

The purification of the throat chakra, within the n*EH*ck, converts us into *EH*missaries who can *EH*xpress* and conv*AY* *EH*mpathy for others and *EH*cstasy for life through sound w*AY*ves. By t*EH*stifying to the truth and persu*AY*ding others to do the same, *EH*choing the s*AY*ges, we b*AY*de farewell to separation and b*EH*ckon w*H*oleness (*H*oliness) to suffuse our being.

Our purity of purpose is centered in the throat chakra, and the effort to release it is the metaphorical dichotomy between *H*eaven and *H*ell.† The re-tuning of this chakra is the fullest emergence of our eternal *H*um, the sound of the true Self.

Our voices are used negatively when we *H*eckle, *H*ector, *H*iss, *H*oot, *H*owl, *H*oller, *H*aggle, *H*arass, *H*arangue, and, in general, get *H*uffy. Taken to extremes, these forms of expression are like placing a *H*ex on someone through *H*atred, *EH*nvy, and *H*ostility, and voicing p*EH*tulant, *H*ysterical, and br*AY*zen expr*EH*ssions that v*EH*nt bad t*EH*mper and ber*AY*te others, gr*AY*ting on their ears. Equally, in failing to listen to others' communications, we turn a d*EH*f ear. A blocked throat chakra f*EH*tters the voice, and instead of speaking forthrightly, we feel inwardly ch*AY*stened and become *H*E*H*sitant, repr*EH*ssed, r*EH*ticent, and *EH*mbarrassed, perhaps even ash*AY*med. This is well expressed in the phrase "*H*emming and *H*awing." Then there are the limiting physical effects when voices become *H*oarse, *H*usky, and *H*acking, or there is an obstruction in the tr*AY*chea.

---

*There are a number of words in English that begin with the syllable "ex," indicative of various kinds and types of communication: exhort, expiate, explain, explicate, extrovert, exude, exult, excuse, exegesis, exert, and excite.

†The word *hell* is paradoxical as it appears as a word for "darkness" in English, but means "light" in German.

9

The Brow Chakra

Sanskrit name:	*Ajna* (Command)*
Location:	Point between the eyebrows
Endocrine gland:	Pineal
Sense:	Clairvoyance
Natural Characteristics:	Clear vision, intuition, insight, introspection, wisdom
Vowels:	*I* (*eye*)† and *IH* as in s*I*t
Consonant:	*SSS*
Tantra seed syllable:	*AUM* or *OM*
Created seed syllable:	*SIM* as in S*I*Mon‡

---

*The brow chakra is known as *ajna,* meaning "command," because it is the recipient of the teacher's (guru's) telepathic communications with his students.
†Also as the consonant *Y* when used as a vowel, as in *psyche* and *mystic.*
‡The term *created* seed syllable is used here rather than *adapted* seed syllable because the Tantra seed syllable *AUM* or *OM* is not adapted. Rather a new syllable has been created based on the pattern of a consonant followed by a vowel and ending with *M*. This also applies to the created seed syllable for the crown chakra. It should also be noted that some branches of Tantra use the seed syllable *KSHAM* for the brow chakra and reserve the *AUM* or *OM* for the crown.

Traditionally this chakra is known as the "third e*Ye*,"* that which can *S*ee beyond the ordinary sense of v*IH*sion. When this chakra is attuned we receive the gifts of *IH*n*S*ight and *IH*ntuition as we *S*can our inner world and *S*tare into the *S*acred *S*anctuary *S*pace of *S*ublime *SI*lence. We become w*I*se *S*ages and *S*oothsayers with pure *IH*ntellect, *IH*ntro*S*pection, and ps*Y*chic abilities. Here, within the brow chakra, is the fullest and br*I*ghtest *IH*nner l*I*ght and *IH*llumination, where the *S*pirit and the *S*oul can reveal their *S*erenity. *S*peculation gives way to *S*urety as gl*IH*mpses of the *S*upreme *S*elf are *S*een.

The w*IH*tness of the third eye becomes aware of the *S*igns, links with universal m*I*nd, and informs the heart, engendering *S*ervice, *S*urrender, and *S*ympathy. In this we emulate Chr*I*st and *S*aint-like qualities. The *I*dea as archetype becomes known in the realm of h*I*gher states of consciousness, the m*IH*sticism of d*IH*vine *IH*magination. In cleansing this chakra, life becomes a *S*acramental r*I*te and *SIH*mplicity itself. The he*I*ghtened *S*ense of the third eye perceives a world rich with *S*ynthesis, *S*ymbiosis, *S*ymbolism, and *S*ymmetry. The fineness of these perceptions is a form of clairvoyance. In such moments, t*I*me and *S*pace stand in *S*tillness and true *S*c*I*ence (knowledge) is revealed.

When the brow chakra is mis-tuned we are victims of *S*piritual bl*I*ndness, a separation that leads to *I*solation and l*I*es about oneself. To have such bl*I*ndness is to live in a world of M*IH*st, m*IH*rages, *I*dols, and m*Y*ness, where the l*I*ght of consciousness has greatly

---

*It is appropriate that the letter *Y* stands at the center of the word *eye,* because it provides a link between the heart and brow chakras. The "eye of the heart" is a well-known spiritual expression.

d*IH*mmed, a dark n*I*ght of the *S*oul, because there is so much gr*IH*t on the m*IH*rror. When this chakra is purified we are no longer under the *S*pell of the metaphorical *S*erpent, or *S*atan, whose *S*hadowy *S*orcery deceives us, bolsters our false pr*I*de, and generally keeps us a*S*leep. This is not unlike the so-called black arts of w*IH*tches and w*IH*zards. A blockage in this chakra could be a h*I*ding and blotting out of something, perhaps a *S*ecret *SIH*n or *S*orrow that bl*I*nds the third eye and precipitates a cr*I*sis. This condition might manifest itself physically as m*I*graine headaches and *SI*nus problems.

10
The Crown Chakra

Sanskrit name:	*Sahasrara* (thousand-petaled)
Location:	Top of the cranium
Endocrine gland:	Pituitary
Sense:	Clairsentience*
Natural Characteristics:	Beingness, liberation, complete fulfillment, contentment, bliss
Vowel:	*EEEE*
Consonants:	*K* (hard C)
Tantra seed syllable:	Beyond sound[†]
Created seed syllable:	*KEEM*

---

*Clairsentience is the special ability of a person to receive psychic knowledge by means of feeling.

[†]In the Tantra tradition, the crown chakra is supposed to be beyond audible sound. This is sometimes described as connected to a particular breathing sound known in Sanskrit as *visarga,* a voiceless aspirant that symbolizes the metaphysical union of the gods Shiva and Shakti. Some Tantra traditions connect it with the *OM*.

At the *C*rown (*C*ranium, *C*ap, *C*rest, *C*rescent, s*K*ull), the p*EE*ak and z*EE*nith of the chakra system, we become as one with the supr*EE*me *CrEE*ator, the *K*yr*EE*e (Greek for Lord) of the *C*hristian liturgy and the *K*ing of glory (*kudos* in Greek), and live in *C*alm, *C*ontented b*EE*ingness. It is the place where *C*osmic or *C*hrist *C*onsciousness can manifest, where the doorway to *EE*ternal life can be opened through the magic *K*E*E*y of grace, and where there can be awareness of the fine *EE*theric substance. Its perfect flowering and whirl allow us to h*EE*d our *C*onscience. The word *conscience* translates literally as "with *K*nowledge." Not ordinary *K*nowledge, but specifically spiritual *K*nowledge, our *K*en,* as symbolized by the silent *K*.† It requires that we have a *K*E*E*nness, z*EE*al, and *EE*agerness to absorb that *K*nowledge. This, in turn, *C*leanses the *C*ausal level, allowing the good s*EE*ds to grow and the useless ones to dissolve. This leads to great moments of unity in which there is no division among spirit, psych*EE*, and pure *EE*go, our individuality. In resonating with this expanded state of *C*onsciousness, our *EE*motions are at their purest and our *EE*volution,‡ *EE*mancipation, fr*EE*dom, and rel*EE*se have the potential to be realized.§ The h*EE*ling process is then well on its

---

*One definition of the word "ken," derived from the German word *kennen* (to know), is "the range of perception, understanding, or knowledge."

†The word *Knowledge* can be broken down into these symbolic themes: *K*= the silent witness, the power (German: *Kraft*) of the *K*yrie (Lord), Now = Being in the present moment, L = Love, and Edge = Living on the edge, where reality and unreality can be distinguished.

‡There are two pronunciations of the word *evolution,* the American sound as *EH* and the chiefly British sound as *EE*.

§In the English pronouns *hEE, shEE,* and *wEE,* there is the sonic implication that men and women, individually and as a collective, have the potential to lead active lives filled with the purest motives when the crown chakra is in the clear.

way and the result is complete *EE*quilibrium and d*EE*p p*EE*ce. In effect, we return to our natural, innate selves, full of m*EE*kness and *K*indness as a newborn child (*Kind* is German for *child,* and *kind* in Old English means "natural, innate"). It is the same state we all enter in d*EE*p sl*EE*p.

The roots of the obstacles that inhibit go quite deep, and even in the upper echelons of the chakra system there can be impediments. One of these tenacious obstacles is the identification with the *C*oarse body—the *C*orporeal and the *C*arnal. To think that we are the body is a fundamental w*EE*kness that inhabits us all. In a sense the body, though honored as the vehicle of *C*onsciousness, has to be *C*rucified. This is the profound meaning of the *C*ross in the life of *C*hrist. When we are fr*EE*d from this *K*not (here the silent *K* represents the last stage of ignorance), then we are aware of all that we are (k)*N*ot, and through this can witness the real and *K*now I Am That.

The deep roots of the impure *EE*go find *C*unning, *C*lever, *C*onniving, and *C*landestine ways of inhibiting the latter stages of liberation and enlightenment. The impure *EE*go does not want to *K*ow-tow to the desire of the Self for liberation. This is the final spiritual *C*risis and it is a subtle *C*orruption of the soul against which we should have the greatest vigilance. When the *C*rown chakra is fully purified we dispel the last *C*louds of un*K*nowing, and thus any possibility of *EE*vil being perpetrated. Any f*EE*lings of Gr*EE*f about separation from our true Self are dispelled. The r*EE*ality of who and what we are dawns on us, and then we have, in the words of *C*hrist, inherited *EE*ternal life.

11

All Chakras and the Consonant *M*

In the Mandukya Upanishad,* one of our great sources of wisdom, it states that the hu*MM*ing *M* is the sound of the true Self.† It is one of the primary sounds that a child first *M*utters, and correspondingly, the word for *mother* begins with the *M* in many languages.

The proposition that the *MMM* is relevant to our true nature was tested by a psychiatrist in Wisconsin who put his schizophrenic patients on a regimen of hu*MM*ing. The result was that for 59 percent of these patients, their hallucinations substantially decreased.[1] In other words, each of those patients was gradually moving closer to his or her true Self and away from the false self living in delusions. So we have the natural fundamental sound of contentment, the hu*M*, as

---

*One of the approximate 108 Upanishads, part of the body of Hindu scriptures. They are a refinement of the spiritual teachings of the ancient Vedas.

†In all the seed syllables, either the original Tantra ones or the adapted ones, *MMM* plays an important role in re-tuning the entire energy system and cannot be confined to just one chakra.

our vibrational supporter that draws us h*OM*e to our true Self, as a *M*other would do with her child. The *MMM* is a sonic *M*assage and bal*M* that engenders a state of cal*M*.

Contentment should be the natural state of *M*ankind (the pure *M*ind of the child). Discontent arises when we claim to be an independent ego, rather than identifying with the true inner *M*aster and *M*aker, the individual (undivided) Self. This undivided Self contains the *M*emory of the spiritual connection with the Divine. It *M*ur*M*urs to us as an inner voice, sending us *M*essages every *M*oment. It shows us that we have the power of a *M*ajestic *M*onarch, as well as the *M*ettle and hu*M*bleness of a *M*onk. The *M*arriage between our divine spark and universal being is always present, and we need to know this *M*erger very consciously. Then we are capable of transmitting the *M*oral and *M*otive force (love) that flows from the *M*agnificent Self.

The true Self is the *M*ediator between our *M*ortal and i*MM*ortal nature. The *M*ysticism and *M*agic of our existence are found in the true Self, and its *M*ystery can be awakened by *M*editation as well as the enchantment of *M*usic and its *M*elodies. Hy*M*ns of praise are a veritable vibrational *M*edicine.

When we are cut off from the contentment natural to the true Self, we become egoistical and it is all about "*M*e, *M*y, and *M*ine."* Then we inhabit a di*M M*urky world of doo*M* and gloo*M*, caught up in a *M*alaise of *M*elancholy and *M*ourning. It leads to such negative qualities as *M*eanness, *M*alice, *M*alevolence, and at its darkest, *M*urder. It is in the awakening to our true nature that we dismiss the false *M*istaken *M*ask of the clouded ego.

---

*This putting of oneself first as a separate ego has entered the language of young people; instead of saying, "James and I are going out," many express it as, "Me and James are going out."

12
Toning Practices for the Chakras

A human being can be likened to a fine musical instrument that must be kept in good condition. In order for a piano to project its beautiful sounds, it has to be tuned regularly and as well as possible. As all of Creation is in a state of vibration, with myriad frequencies, it follows that the principle of resonance is a fundamental modality for healing, using sympathetic vibrations that mirror what is to be healed. The object is to get the receiver, in this case the chakras, to recognize their sonic nature by sending out specific frequencies to which they will attune. This process is a kind of vocal homeopathy based on the principle that "like cures like."

The most effective and immediate resonator we have is the voice. However, the chief obstacle in using the voice as the resonator is the very thing we want to alter—our psychology. There are many who are not comfortable with their voices or their breathing, and are reluctant to make sounds other than ordinary speech. In such cases it is necessary to overcome the limiting idea that they cannot be self-empowering, and thus self-healing. While it is helpful to work with an alternative health practitioner at times, it is more effective to take control of the healing process on a daily basis through toning. The way through the obstacle lies in the heart's desire for change, and with that the suspension of judgment about one's voice. When the intent is sincere, the real Self responds. For it is not the quality or power of the voice that matters, but a great desire for change. When that is present, the chakra will respond no matter how inadequate the voice might seem to be. For those who would like to improve their voice quality, appendix I offers some basic exercises in warming up the voice and supporting the breath.

TONING THE VOWELS

In the practice of toning the vowels, these little packets of sound become as mantras leading to inner-sound meditation. The process is in two phases: external and internal. The audible, external sound, which can be subdivided into the normal voice and the breath, is the active, awakening, and stimulating phase. It is where the healing juices of the vowels are being extracted and stirred, and establishing a rhythm that eventually takes root in the mind. The more grit there is impeding the chakras, the more we must do this vocal scrubbing—the rhythmic repetition of these mini-mantras.

The inaudible, internal sound occurring within higher mind* is the passive, refining, and deepening phase. Here we rest within the

---

*Higher mind is that part of the Self that transcends the impurities of the ego imposed on the mind.

sound. The latter phase then becomes a form of mantra meditation. This practice is similar to what is known in India as *nada* yoga, meaning "union through inner sound."* All vocal sound healing that we do for ourselves naturally leads to the state of meditation where the deepest healing takes place. It allows us to rest the voice, become passive, and let the higher mind take over the healing vibrations. This is also the view of Dr. Gerber, as succinctly expressed in his book, *Vibrational Medicine:*

> Meditation is an important method of opening, activating, and cleansing the chakras of the body, especially when practiced in conjunction with active forms of visualization.[1]

To this could be added, "in conjunction with active forms of toning."

Each vowel is sounded in a pulsating manner with the option of varying speeds for each chakra. The principle is that the throbbing of the vowels emulates the source of the chakra vibration that is to be resonated, awakened, and re-tuned. The effect is greater than just sustaining the vowel. The pulsations are slight vocal accentuations on a continuous sound, not short staccato bursts, and can be done in groups of seven pulses followed by a silent eighth pulse to allow for new breath intake. Placing the breath *H* on just the first utterance of the vowel at the beginning of each cycle lubricates the sound for smoothness. The volume should not be loud but in a medium voice. In the next stage (a new group of eight pulses),

---

*Nada yoga is union with a subtle sound emanating from the heart that becomes audible and separate from the beating of the heart or a ringing in the ears.

decrease the volume as the sound is drawn inside you. In the final optional stage, whisper the pulsating vowel on the breath. It is optional because your intuition might direct you to give over to the internal process before reaching the whispering breath aspect. You'll need to test the waters and find your own rhythm. The following is the pattern for the heart:

HAH—AH—AH—AH—AH—AH—AH—intake of breath
1   2   3   4   5   6   7   8

The new cycle starts: *HAH—AH,* etc. and so on
1   2

There are two options with regard to the speed of the pulse. One is to choose something that is moderate and comfortable for all the chakras. This could be between 60 and 72 beats per minute (bpm), as measured by a musical metronome.* Alternatively, the speed could be related proportionately to the increasing number of petals, or energy vortices, of the chakras. Varying the speed provides a psychological effect mirroring the ascent through the chakras. These recommended speeds (see chart on page 61), which have no proportional correlations with the number of petals other than the fact that there is increase in number, are set up in increments of 12.

The 40 bpm given in parentheses for the root chakra is the slowest tempo on a metronome, and is therefore the practical starting

---

*The metronome, a device that can be set at varying speeds to measure beats per minute, is often used by musicians to assist in keeping steady time throughout a piece of music.

point, rather than the theoretical 36. The increments are based on an average heartbeat of 72 bpm and the symbolic Vedic number 108, which represents the mid-region between heaven and earth, the equal number of steps from the material world to the realm of divine reality.[2] These two numbers helped to establish the basis for creating an equal division between all the chakras of 12 bpm.

PULSATION SPEEDS FOR TONING WITH VOWELS

Chakra	Pulsations per Minute	Number of Petals
Root	36(40)	4
Sacral	48	6
Solar plexus	60	10
Heart	72	12
Throat	84	16
Brow	96	96
Crown	108	1000

🪷 Finding a Tone

Chakras are attuned to the frequencies of the vowels themselves, and not to particular notes on the scale that the voice produces. So it is not necessary to tone on a low note because the focus is on the lower chakras, or on a high note for the upper chakras. There are four options for what notes could be used:

1. Choose intuitively a comfortable note to be used for all of the chakras. Just allow a tone to emerge in the moment. This is the easiest approach.

2. Use a particular note for all the chakras, one you predetermine by discovering a fundamental tone for yourself. See appendix II for finding such a tone.

3. Focusing on individual chakras, direct your attention to the region of a particular chakra and then choose the note intuitively. Do not be concerned if there are repetitions of certain notes rather than seven unique notes.

4. Use fixed notes in the form of a rising scale. This provides the psychological effect of moving upward through the centers. The recommended scale is the pentatonic beginning on F. See appendix III.

Working with the Sound

Once the pulsations of the vowel are well established, begin to diminish the volume to very soft. At this point, maintain the rhythm and switch to sounding the vowel on just the breath with no tone audible. As noted earlier, the breath phase is transitional and optional and would not last for more than a minute. There will then come an intuitive moment where you cease making the effort and give over to the internal phase in which the pulsating sound has become established in the mind and you surrender to it, passively listening to its rhythm.

The mantric sound should have fixed itself within the mind and taken on a life of its own, unrelated to the heartbeat or the breath. Listen to what you have projected into your consciousness and make no attempt to control it. The breath gap will have disappeared and it will be a continuous throbbing sound at a speed that might well change to either slower or faster. The higher mind knows what is best. All that has to be done is to follow the sound with fullest attention. Should the external phase not have taken hold within, either restart the audible process or make a temporary mental effort to establish the sound as you remember its external form.

The attention is solely on the inner sound and there is no need to place your attention on the chakra in question, which would split your focus. If you are distracted by mental chatter, the first recommendation is to just return your focus to the throbs of sound. If the distractions have carried the mind too far off, try to remember what the sound was and restart it with a gentle mental effort.

There can come a point where your inner sound fades and the pulse becomes very faint. This is an ideal state. There is no need to take note of your breathing or focus on it. Normally, it will slow down. When the sound and the underlying pulse actually disappear, you are experiencing healing at its deepest level. The greatest achievement is to hold the attention on this silence of fullness with a clear mind.

The duration for the entire ritual can range from from fifteen to thirty minutes. For every minute that the active phase consumes, there can be a corresponding passive phase of at least three minutes. Thus, five minutes of external sound could be followed by at least fifteen minutes of internal vibrations. No definitive rules can be given about duration, other than that using only one sound in a given session, the whole process does not extend beyond thirty minutes, even if the process has to be restarted. The external phase should not exceed seven minutes.

❀ Position of the Body

The simplest way to take up this practice is to be on a chair, on the floor, or on a bed, with the back straight without being rigid. For the chair position, choose one that is armless and upright for the back, and keep feet flat on the floor. For the floor, those skilled in yoga and the lotus posture can assume this position. Others could use an ergonomic kneeling chair designed for meditation, or support the back with a wall. When sitting on a bed, pillows can be used to support the back. Whatever is chosen, it is essential that the body be as comfortable and warm as possible, with a straight but not rigid spine. To keep out visual distractions, eyes are closed with an inner focus between the eyebrows. The hands can rest in each other or on the thighs, palms up, as a gesture of receiving from above.

TONING THE CONSONANTS

The consonants *L, V, R, Y, H, S, K,* and *M** are drawn largely from the seed syllables of Tantra. The *L* through *H* consonants are extracted from the first five Tantric syllables for the chakras, as explained in chapter 3. The *S* and *K* have been intuitively assigned to the brow and crown chakras respectively. The *M* has great power as the concluding sound of all the seeds. The aim of using these consonants as sound entities in their own right is to gain more of their healing juices. It is comparable to extracting

---

*A handy mnemonic device to help with remembering the order of consonants from the root up through the crown, excluding the *M*, is: *L*et *V*enus *R*ule *Y*our *H*eart *S*o *K*ind.

the vitamins and minerals from foods to obtain a concentrated form.

The practices with the consonants are described as sound rituals because the word *ritual* is derived from the Sanskrit word *rita,* meaning "universal order and harmony." These rituals can be done for their own sake and benefit, but will also help to intensify the consonant when used as part of the complete Tantra seed. The consonants, like consorts, are the complementary aspect to the vowels for toning the chakras. They are not refined like the vowels with their overtones, but they are effective in their power to cut through deep-rooted impediments.

The following ways of toning the consonants are twofold, one that includes movements and sometimes a concluding sound, and one quite similar to that of toning the vowels. The movements created for this toning are to inspire, encourage, and direct the intention of the ritual.

Movements are very suitable for group work. Matters of duration, numbers of cycles, which notes if any, and what to do following each of these rituals will be given after all of their descriptions.

Ritual for Toning the *L* Consonant (Root Chakra)

The meridians within the human body as given in Chinese medicine have two major channels. The yin channel starts at the perineum, travels up the front of the body, and ends at the tip of the tongue. The yang channel begins at the same place, goes up through the spine into the brain, and ends at the roof of the mouth. These two circuits can be linked by placing the tip of the tongue to the mouth's roof. The whole circuit is sometimes called the "microcosmic orbit."[3] This is exactly what happens when the *L,* pronounced as *AL, EL,* or *UL,* is sounded. The tongue's tip rises up to meet the mouth's roof. Thus it is possible to circulate the energy around the microcosmic orbit while engaged in this ritual. Perhaps the Muslims understand this power subconsciously when they intone the great Allah. It is very noticeable that they put strong emphasis on the sound of the *L* in *Allah.* The pulsations will be done on the sound of *UL* as in "ultimate." Do it slowly so each *UL* takes about four seconds, each sounding having a slight accent. Imagine the tongue to be a shovel digging into the earth as it moves to the roof of the mouth. *L* represents the earth element. As follows:

ULLL ULLL ULLL ULLL and so on (LAH)

With Movement

Take a standing position with one foot slightly forward and the other off to the side, so that the two feet almost create a ninety-degree angle. While pulsating the *L* sound, bend over the front leg as though you want to scoop up some earth. Bend forward only as far as your body will allow. Take the earth in your hands and lift it up. As your hands reach the level of the face, turn them over so that the earth falls out. Carry the hands on up above the head, palms facing the heavens on either side of the body. At this point the pulsation phase ends and a *LAH* is produced on a descending sliding sound to the bottom of your voice. During this slide, let the hands come down in a circular motion and stop in front of the genitals. Here hold a small ball of energy with your hands. This is the active part of a cycle.

While in this passive position holding the ball, very quietly and slowly pulsate the *L* to yourself, holding the tongue to the roof of the mouth. It is under the breath like a kind of muttering. The throbbing of the sound is whatever you feel and does not have to conform to the full voice version. During this phase the microcosmic orbit can be put into practice. That is, hold the tongue in place at the roof of the mouth and experience a flow of energy beginning with the eyes, moving down the front of the body to the tailbone and then up the spine and into the head. One circuit equals one sounding of *UL*.

Without Movement

Sit as you would for toning the vowels. Do the full strength *UL* repetitions as above, without the *LAH* conclusion, and alternate with the slow, quiet pulsations while enacting the microcosmic orbit.

❀ Ritual for Toning the V Consonant (Sacral Chakra)

In order to squeeze all the juice from the *V*, use the syllable *VIV*, as in the name "Vivian." Start by slowing pronouncing *VIV* on any tone that emerges from your voice. Feel a buzzing sensation on your lips. Gradually allow it to become faster and faster until it feels as though all that occurs are buzzing lips. This is preliminary to having the full flavor of the sound. Maintain the fast speed during the full-voice phase of the cycle. In the passive phase, just slowly and quietly mumble *VIV* on the lips under the breath.

VIV VIV VIV VIV VIV and so on

With Movement

The movement, indicating the energy field around this chakra, is in a standing position. Hold the hands just off the body over where the pockets of trousers would be. The fingers are somewhat pointing toward each other. Move the hands toward each other as they come in front of the sacral region, and just before the fingers touch, push the hands in parallel outward about a foot. At that point turn the palms downward and slowly make a semicircle movement back to their original position. It is as though you are spreading the sound over the aura of the chakra. All this is done while sounding the *VIV* aloud. During the quiet sound, hold the hands in their original position before starting the next cycle.

Without Movement

Sitting as for the vowels, follow the pattern of the active and passive sounding of *VIV* as given above.

❀ Ritual for Toning the R Consonant (Solar Plexus Chakra)

The sound to be produced is *ERR,* as in the word *ERRor.* By using this sound we vibrate out of the solar plexus all that is, in fact, error. The sound should have a fiery edge to it, almost approaching a growl. It is a sound of slowly burning anger. Pulsate the sound, beginning easily and allowing it to grow louder during the active part of each cycle.

ERRR ERRR ERRR ERRR ERRR and so on *(RAH)*

With Movement

Stand comfortably and hold out your hands palms up at navel level, as if you are to receive something. As the sound begins, slowly move the hands toward the solar plexus so that the palms are facing the navel. It is as though you are going to pull something out of the solar plexus, like removing a diseased organ. Then lift the hands up and out, palms facing upward, so that they reach the level of the forehead. Once there, thrust the hands downward rigorously to the level of the navel, as though throwing out all the rubbish through the arms and hands.

Accompany this thrust, releasing the *ERRR* sound, with a sliding, descending *RAH* to the bottom of the voice. In the passive phase hold the hands in the receiving position at the level of the navel and very quietly murmur the pulsating *ERRR* to yourself. This is the simmering phase before the sound returns to the full-voice boiling phase.

Without Movement

Sitting as for vowels, alternate between the active and passive phases as given above and without the use of the sliding *RAH*.

Ritual for Toning the Y Consonant (Heart Chakra)

The letter *Y* is an ambivalent consonant, as it also functions as a vowel in English. Attempts to sustain it very quickly turn into an *EE* vowel at the beginning of a word. So in this ritual it is necessary to combine the *Y* with vowels. The two sounds chosen are *YAH* and *YOO,* both of which will be sounded as descending slides of the voice. There is a benefit in using the sliding in that we are offering our bodies a multiplicity of frequencies from which to take vibrational nourishment.

With Movement

Place one hand near the thymus (between the lungs, center of the upper sternum) with the fingers in a tapping position. This is the active hand. The other hand is passive and should hover just above the active hand. Firmly tap on the thymus with the active hand.* After about fifteen seconds, slow the tapping and then press the fingers into the chest. This tapping also symbolizes that you are opening the heart, cutting a pathway for pure love to emerge. The pressing of the fingers provides a sense of release when the hand lets go.

After this thymus stimulation, produce the *YAH* sound, stretching the *Y* as much as possible before moving to the *AH* and doing it on a relatively high note so as to be able to slide the voice downward. At the same time, lift both hands above the head as though you are holding a large ball above you, and look up at it. Then allow a few moments for another breath. With the next vocalization, the downward sliding *YOO,* make a gesture with the outstretched hands that is one of a very large embrace, as though you want to pull an enormous being into your heart. At the close the hands come to rest on the heart, one above the other. While in

---

*The corresponding gland for the heart chakra is the thymus, the master gland for the immune system. Some kinesiologists and practitioners of the Emotional Freedom Technique recommend gently tapping the thymus with the fingers to stimulate the gland's secretions.

this resting position follow the breath, mentally taking in a non-sliding *YAH* through the nose and sending out mentally through the mouth a non-sliding *YOO*. It as though you are breathing in and out of the heart.

Without Movement

Sitting as for vowels, hold the hands on the heart and alternatively sound the *YAH* and *YOO* slowly as straight tones. Following this, do it mentally as given above.

⊛ Ritual for Toning the *H* Consonant (Throat Chakra)

For the production of the *H* breath sound, widen the mouth and open the throat as though an orange has been placed inside the oral cavity. Produce a very full-throated breath sound on *HA* with this mouth position. It should feel like a cleansing action, almost like a kind of gargle. Create intensity of sound by supporting it with strong abdominal contractions. The duration is not important but the intensity is.

With Movement

Begin in a good seated position. For the movement, fully extend your arms and hands out in front of you, shoulder height. On the in-breath, slowly draw the hands toward the shoulders, allowing the arms to bend close to the body, elbows pointing down. With the sounding of the *H* consonant, very slowly push the hands back to the original position. Keep repeating this two-fold simple movement. Upon completion of these cycles, spend a little time just following your breath as it flows in through the nose and gently out through the mouth.

Without Movement

Sitting as for vowels, follow the above description without moving the arms.

⊛ Ritual for Toning the S Consonant (Brow Chakra)

This sound is a hiss (*SSSSS*) and vibrates the head region. It is very much held within the mouth, with only a small aperture of the lips to allow for the escaping air. The ritual is adapted from procedures of the Taoist tradition of medicine, which uses highly specific sounds for relieving stress from the organs of the body. In this case, mentally direct the sound as though it is being sent through the brow chakra as a cleansing force.

With Movement

Begin by sitting at the edge of a chair with erect back posture. Focus your attention between the eyebrows with eyes closed. Your hands, with palms up, rest upon your lap. On a long in-breath, slowly lift your hands until they reach the level of the forehead. The hands then swivel around so that the palms face outward, the middle fingers almost touching and roughly parallel with the eyebrows. On the out-breath, sounding the *SSS*, slowly push the hands out, extending them to arm's length. Upon completion of the sound, lower the hands to the lap and maintain a very quiet SSS before doing the next cycle.

Without Movement

Follow the instructions above with no movement of the arms.

🧠 Ritual for Toning the *K* Consonant (Crown Chakra)

The consonant *K* (or hard *C*) is an explosive sound in our language. Just before its sound is emitted the throat locks, and then the unlocking burst of vibration follows. It has the quality of cutting through something that is hard and resistant. Its very shape hints at its properties. Consider the vertical line as a target, and the two angular lines as an arrow piercing that target (see diagram below).

Interestingly, the very implement for *Cutting* (hard *C*) is a *K*nife (silent *K*). It is in a *C*risis that something in our *C*onsciousness breaks through, and why people wanting to release strong pent-up emotions will use the name of *C*hrist. To unlo*CK* the lo*CK,* there needs to be a *K*ey.

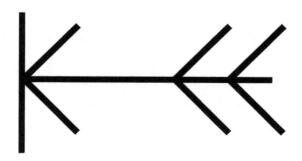

Illustration of the letter K as described just above.

So first have the experience of the locking and unlocking of the throat. Mentally, start its sound but do not allow it to come out for a few seconds. Then unlock the throat and release the sound. Do this a few times and then produce a strong explosive *K*. It should be a pure *K* and not with an added *AH* as in *KA*. It is like a throat sneeze. Thereafter discontinue the locking/unlocking preliminary. After the initial explosion, allow the residue of the *K* sound to reverberate in the throat, and mentally direct it down the spinal column. The emotion is of both spiritual power (as in the German word for power—*Kraft*) and release. The Mayans had a toning practice on the sound *K'IN* (divided into *K* and *EEN*) for just such a purpose.[4]

Partly because the *K* reverberation is not long, it is appropriate to follow the *K* with a vowel, in this instance *EE,* also associated with the crown, as a descending siren sound. Starting somewhat high in the voice, create a pure *EE* vowel, like wailing* rather than screaming. Let the sound drop slowly all the way down to the very bottom of the voice. Each of these sounds, the *K* and the *EE,* requires its own breath.

With Movement

In a standing position, place one foot forward and the other off to the side so that the two feet almost form a 90-degree angle. Uplift the hand, palm upturned, that corresponds to the forward foot. This is the hand of asking (the word *asK* ending with *K*), and should form a cup so that it would be possible to pour a little water into it. The

---

*The sliding sound of *EEE* as a form of wailing, or "keening," is practiced in Ireland by women at wakes. It is an expression of grief and a way of restoring energy depleted by the loss of a loved one.

other hand is placed palm up on the side of the body at waist level. This is a kind of fencer's position where the weight is on the forward foot. The eyes are focussed on the uplifted hand. In this position, explode the *K* with its residue sound down the spine.

Taking a second breath, sound the *EE* and begin to slide it slowly down. At the same time lower the hand above, moving it in a straight line toward the hand at the waist. Look deeply into the moving hand's palm as though you are being drawn into it. In the process the knees should bend, and your weight gradually shift to the back foot. Once the moving hand falls into the stationary hand, the sound is completed and you should look as though you are bowing to a queen, your eyes still looking into the hand. While in this resting position, close your eyes and follow your breath. To restart another cycle, slowly lift the moving hand upward to its original position, following its ascent with your eyes.

In the sitting version with movement, sit comfortably in a chair. The hands—palms up, one above the other—will be resting in the center of the body. Raise the upper hand keeping the palm upward, which will take it slightly off to the side of the body. Look at this hand as it rises and keep focused on it. Create the explosive *K* with its residue sound. On the siren *EE* let the raised hand slowly descend and fall back into the palm of the other hand. Again, follow the hand movement with the eyes. With the head in a normal position, close your eyes and follow your breath until starting up the next cycle.

Without Movement

In a sitting position as with vowels, enact the ritual without any movement. A choice here is to eliminate the *EE* vowel and do only a series of explosive *K* sounds, with the residue sound.

⚜ Ritual for Toning the *M* Consonant (All Chakras)

The humming *M* consonant is central to all the seed syllables of Tantra, forming their third aspect. Thus, it is applicable to all the chakras. It is the great antidote to anxiety and the hallmark of contentment. In effect, the humming *M* empowers our self-esteem and individuality because its sound calms and purifies the soul. In the Upanishads it is synonymous with the real Self.

Humming is a natural sound and needs no description of how to produce it. Keep the lips relaxed and maintain a moderate volume. As you approach the end of the humming ritual, decrease the volume, moving toward silence. There are three ways to enhance the efficacy of the hum. It is your choice to use none, some, or all of these options. Let experience be your guide in the early stages.

1. Smile slightly. This gesture corresponds to the contentment that is being engendered by the hum. It is similar to the inner smile of the Taoist healing tradition, which is related to the stimulation of the thymus gland and endorphins. Feel the smile in your eyes and ever so slightly in the corners of your mouth.

2. Direct the hum and the smile to the central point of Self between the heart and the throat. Optionally, the hands can be held on the body over this point of Self, keeping the arms relaxed.

3. The hum can be pulsated by using a slight, gentle chewing action. It is just possible to maintain the smile and do this. This would be in keeping with the process of toning the vowels as described previously.

Keep the mind focused on the central point of Self and catch breaths as you require them, as it is a continuous sound. After about five minutes, draw the outer humming to a close, listen for any inner pulsations, and keep your attention on the point of Self. In this meditative state the hands may be removed from the upper chest and placed in the lap.

General Guidelines for Toning Consonants

The suggestions for choosing tones and determining how long to maintain them are broad guidelines. You will get a better sense of these as you begin to work regularly with them.

Choosing Notes

There are four consonants that have an actual sounding note: *L, V, R,* and *M.* As with the vowels, let your intuition guide you and be spontaneous in allowing whatever note emerges. Undoubtedly it will be in the relaxed low-to-middle range of the voice. Keep open to the intuition because it is possible to change the note during all the cycles of a given consonant. It can be deliberate if the initial note feels uncomfortable for whatever reason.

Sliding Sound

Begin these sounds high enough so that there is a reasonable distance through which to descend. Go right down to the very bottom of the voice.

Time Period after Toning

Essentially it is natural and right to go into a meditation after toning, be it a vowel, consonant, or seed syllable. This means that if you have chosen to do the consonant toning with movement in a standing position, you'll need to sit down. So if you will be using a chair, have it just behind you. Where there is a definitive pulsation involved (*L, V, R, H*), place your attention at the appropriate chakra point while listening for any inner pulsations that might have been created by the toning repetitions. For the remaining ones (*Y, S, K, M*) there are two options: the one just given and the following of the breath. In the former it is possible that even though pulsations were not applied externally, the toning process has nonetheless stimulated inner pulsations. Following the breath as a form of meditation has long been established in various traditions, and the toning should have had the effect of slowing it down. Always be guided by your intuition here.

Duration

It is far better to measure the duration of each ritual by minutes, rather than numbers of cycles. It is easy to forget how many cycles have been done. The actual sounding should be from five to ten minutes. In less than five minutes the sound might not have taken root. More than ten minutes and the physical action can become tiring. The duration of the succeeding silence is in your hands. In total the two phases, external and internal, should not exceed a half-hour. This will also depend on what daily regimen you choose (see the end of this chapter).

TONING SEED SYLLABLES

Tantra seed syllables—the bija mantras—contain threefold sounds consisting of an opening consonant, a central vowel, and the closing hum of *M*. Therefore, in order to fully extract and absorb the juices of all three elements, it is best to work with a slow to moderate speed.* An effective way of producing them is in sets of five repetitions followed by a breath. However, because of the slowness of the pulse and the final *M,* it is likely that a second breath will be necessary, perhaps before the fifth repetition. Extend in particular the opening consonant, which usually goes by quickly. On the fifth repetition of the cycle, extend the *M* for a few seconds before proceeding to the next cycle. All the seed sounds are done in the same way up to the fifth chakra. As follows for the original seed syllable for the root chakra:

LLAHMM LLAHMM LLAHMM LLAHMM LLAHMMMMMM

The production of the vowel in the five original seed syllables is found in the opening sound of the words *alms* and *almond*. There are two choices for each chakra, as given in the outlines about them in chapter 4—the original form from Tantra and the adapted Western form. In the latter, the consistent central vowel is replaced with the different vowels. Furthermore, new seed syllables are introduced for the brow and crown chakras. In summary:

---

*A recommended speed for the seed syllable repetitions is from 60 to 72 bpm (metronome marking). Each of the first four repetitions will receive four such beats, and the last repetition with the extended *MMM* will have eight. The recorded examples have a median speed of 66 bpm.

SUMMARY OF ORIGINAL
AND ADAPTED SEED SYLLABLES

Chakra	Tantra	Adapted Western
Root	LAM	LUHM (as in *lump*)
Sacral	VAM	VOOM (as in *voodoo*)
Solar	RAM	RAWM (as in *raw*)
Heart	YAM	YAHM (as in *yacht*)
Throat	HAM	HAYM (as in *hay*)
Brow	OM	SIM (as in *Simon*)
Crown	MMM	KEEM (as in *keen*)

In Tantra it is the consonants that direct the sounds to the corresponding chakras, with the central vowel opening up the heart energy and the closing hum bringing a refining resonance to all the chakras. In the adapted Western version, the vibrations are tilted in favor of the individual chakras, as both the consonant and the vowel are directed into the energy centers.*

The sounding of *OM* is not divided into sets but is continual, separated only by short breaths. Once you see the length of your out-breath for *OM,* ensure that equal amounts of time are given to the *O* and the *M.* The humming *MMM* for the crown can be done as described in the earlier section on consonants.

Upon completion of the external sound, whether doing one or more of the chakras at a time, move your consciousness into inner

---

*Appendix IV contains a whole series of consonant/vowel combinations whereby the consonant sound of one chakra is elided with the vowel sound of another. This is a way of condensing the toning for working on two chakras simultaneously.

space and focus your attention at the base of the spine. Listen for any pulsations that have arisen. This is the releasing of your dormant, natural mantra. As noted with regard to the vowels, this throbbing (assuming it occurs) is essentially a rhythmic feeling and is unrelated to the heartbeat or the breath. Do not expect that the pulsations will be at the same speed at which the seed syllables were produced. There is every potential that they will eventually fade away into a fullness of silence, to which our attention remains directed. All the guidelines for toning the vowels—the choosing of the notes, restarting, and the sitting positions—apply to the seed syllables. As always, volume should be moderate. The duration of the process should not exceed a half-hour. If you are working with individual chakras, a maximum of seven minutes should be sufficient, followed by inner sound/silence. If toning all of them in succession, approximately two minutes can be given to each (fourteen minutes total), and then the inner sound/silence up to sixteen minutes.

Regimens for Toning

It would seem that toning the seed syllables would be one's first option because they contain both the vowels and consonants. However, choices are not only logical but also emotional, so it is only through experimentation that you will discover which choices you will pursue. All three (vowel, consonant, and syllables) can be practiced. In addition, there is the choice of which chakras to address. If you are not dominated or plagued by particular negative psychological states, then toning all seven would seem right as a practice for general well-being. On the other hand, you can focus on the chakras that hold within them the negative traits that inhibit you.

Many traditions of meditation practice suggest that it be done twice a day for twenty to thirty minutes each sitting. The usual times are morning before breakfast and evening before dinner. This would apply equally to the toning and inner sound meditations.

Here are some examples for a half-hour session:

1. For one chakra, five minutes using any choice followed by fifteen minutes of inner meditation.
2. For one chakra, five minutes on the pure vowel or consonant followed by ten minutes of inner sound. Then five minutes on the seed syllable followed by ten minutes of inner sound.
3. For two chakras, as above except shifting the second half procedure to another chakra.

Whether you work with one or more of the chakras, you could alternate the vowels and consonants with each succeeding day in the morning, and do just seed syllables in the evening. As there are seven days in a week, this is perfect if toning all seven chakras. For example:

OUTLINE FOR A DAILY REGIMEN

	Morning	Evening
Day 1	Vowel	Seed syllable
Day 2	Consonant	Seed syllable

And so on.

Alternately, you could do a vowel/seed syllable combination in the morning and a consonant/seed syllable in the evening. Also vowel/vowel, consonant/consonant, or vowel/consonant. Part of the process of self-healing is to design your own program according to your needs and how you see yourself. With these regimens it does not need to be prescriptive.

Finally, if you wish to do all seven chakras in succession at one sitting, it is best to use only the seed syllables. Vowels and consonants take more time to unfold before going into inner space, so confine yourself to no more than two in a thirty-minute session.

More resources for your practice can be found in the following appendices. As always, let your intuition be your guide.

Preliminary Exercises for the Voice

The following exercises are offered for those who would like to improve the quality of their voices—for those who feel that there is tension in their sound or their breath lacks support. This is no requirement that these exercises be put into practice before taking up the toning.

GIBBERISH

A very simple way of opening up the voice and, at the same time, loosening the jaw and tongue is to improvise nonsensical speech and sounds. Often known as "gibberish," it breaks through inhibitions and opens a gateway to vocal freedom. It is a known mind-clearing ritual in certain ashrams in India. In creating these sounds, exaggerate the jaw and tongue movements, be enthusiastic in getting your imaginary points across, and bring hand and arm gestures into play. The rest is up to you. Obviously it works well with a partner when both persons are speaking at once. Three to five minutes are sufficient.

RELAXATION AND OPENING THE THROAT

This exercise is quite similar to the act of gargling, in which the throat is naturally opened to allow the liquid to go as far back as possible. The object is to speak the following syllables deep at the back of the throat without moving the jaw or tongue.

GUNG GANG GING

First, shape the mouth with the mouth wide open as though it contains a whole orange. Do not stretch the jaw to where it feels tense. Keep the tongue completely still, sitting at the bottom of the mouth. Then, having the sense of gargling and without raising your head, take one of the above syllables and attempt to sound it deep in the throat in slow repetitions. After the short burst of the syllable, a humming tone will appear between each re-sounding. This will be like a sung tone but the actual syllable should not be. It is essentially a spoken sound. Take each syllable in turn for about a minute each. Eventually you can move through the three as a set, seeing how flexible your throat region is in changing the vowel. Following the repetitive slowly spoken syllables (whether working with a single one or the set), send out a real sung note on *HOO,* feeling the note emerging from the place where the vocal gargling was done. These sounds are demonstrated on the CD accompanying this book.

BREATHWORK

There are two primary aspects in the process of breathing: the relaxation of the diaphragm on the intake of breath to allow for maximum capacity of air within, and the finely controlled contractions of the abdominal region for the out-breath. The first step is to practice the movement fully relaxing the belly by releasing any tension there, and/or purposefully stretching the muscles. For the out-breath the aim is to control the muscle contractions of the belly as finely as possible so that it almost feels as though there is hardly any inward movement of the belly. Although not possible, imagine the belly button moving toward and eventually touching the spine. This is a description of what can be called "belly breathing," as there has been no mention of the lungs at all. In practicing these movements, allow the breath to do as it wishes. In fact, the breath could stand still during this preparatory exercise.

For the intake of air in this context, the mouth will be used. However, this is not a recommendation for breathing in everyday life. On the contrary, it is essential that we breathe through the nose so that the energy of *prana* in the air reaches the head region. Mouth breathing is specifically confined to doing independent breathwork. The idea is that the air is imagined as a liquid being sipped down into the belly. That is, the air is being drunk through a straw. In doing this, imagine that you are a balloon that expands with the intake of air. In balloon blowing, the air is pushed down to the furthest point and then fills up.

In a standing position, place your hands lightly on the belly so as to feel the experience. Begin by relaxing and stretching the abdominal muscles as the receptacle for the air. Suck or sip the air in through the mouth and direct it to the lowest reaches of the belly. Do the intake either as one continuous breath or a series of smaller breaths, and fill up at your own speed. Experimentation is needed here. When you have filled the belly so that it feels "bloated," change over to the out-breath. In the first stage, pucker your lips as though blowing out a candle and produce a steady stream of air controlled by the fine contractions of the abdomen. In subsequent stages go on to produce an actual vowel sound of *OH* or *OO* or *AH* at a reasonable volume. Between each attempt, take time out and follow your nose breathing, observing the movements of the abdomen. Do not expect immediate results regarding the duration and quality of the vocal sounds. Only consistent practicing over several days will produce a noticeable difference.

After a time of keeping the hands on the belly, the following movements could help encourage the process. In a well-balanced standing position, use your hands to form and hold a ball of energy and place the ball in front of the throat. While drawing in the air through the mouth, bring the ball down slowly to waist level and once there, pull the ball apart by moving the hands away from each other and just beyond the body frame. All this movement corresponds to the descent of the air and expansion of the belly. Adjust the speed of this movement in succeeding attempts so that just at the end with separated hands, the intake reaches completion. Hold this position for a few seconds and then send out a vowel sound on any note. During the sound, slowly draw the hands back together at the waist to re-form the ball. To parallel the contractions producing the vowel, imagine a resistance between the hands like two opposing magnets, so that the hands move slowly as though having something to overcome. When the breath is expended, spend time following your nose breathing and again observing the movement of the abdomen. When you are ready for the next cycle, very slowly move the ball of energy back up to the front of the throat.

Discovering Your Fundamental Tone

Initially, to be able to determine what your fundamental tone might be, a recording device and/or some kind of well-tuned piano keyboard is required. An electronic keyboard of two octaves (twenty-five notes) would be sufficient. Begin in a very relaxed position, either sitting or lying down. Follow your breathing for a couple of minutes. Next, form with your lips the shape for sounding the vowel *OO*. At first you send through the lips only the breath sound of *OO*. Do at least three breath-only emissions before allowing any actual note to appear in the voice. Be as gentle as possible until the vocal cords create a tension that changes the pure out-breath sound into an actual note. The feeling has to be that you are not doing it, but rather it is doing itself. Once this note quietly emerges, stay with it and slightly increase the volume. Proceed as follows:

Record the tone you produce, holding on to it as long as possible. A recording would give much time afterward to determine what the note is. Otherwise, the note produced will have to be regularly sounded while searching for its name. While playing back the recording or continuing to hold the tone, search for the matching note on the keyboard. For a woman, start with middle C (see keyboard diagram below), and for a man, the C that is eight white notes (one octave) lower (to the left). First move your finger to the left down the keyboard, note-by-note, including all the black notes. Go no more than a distance of five white keys. The object is to find a note that you believe corresponds to the note you are projecting. It is equally possible that your note might be higher from where you started with your finger. So then return to that starting note and go up (to the right) note-by-note. Again, go up no more than five white keys. Within this range of nine white keys and six black keys above and below the starting C should be your note. Write down that note as indicated in the diagram below:

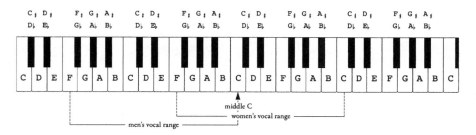

Two-octave piano keyboard diagram with added letter-names of notes.

This whole procedure could be done three times for each session. Undertake at least five sessions in determining what your fundamental tone is. On this basis you would have fifteen tones recorded and notated. In fact, fifteen tones is a good minimum number for making a choice. You are seeking a tone that reappears at least two-thirds of the time. So in this case, ten tones would be identical. If this does not feel satisfactory, more than five sessions could be done. Because of the relaxed state of the voice, the note will be middle to low in the voice, and that is as it should be. The process of capturing this fundamental tone is not an easy one, and requires sensitive hearing and patience. Remember that it is not necessary to discover one overriding note within you. It is just one possibility in toning the chakras.

Using a Musical Scale
for Toning

It is highly unlikely that there is one universal scale of tones for every person that represents the seven-step ascent through the chakras. Therefore, any choice for such a scale is purely psychological and subjective. Among practitioners the usual recommended scale is our Western one of C major, containing seven tones equal to the seven chakras. The choice of C major is understandable; because it uses only white keys (no sharps or flats). The starting note C is situated at the center point of the keyboard, and it is the first scale that musicians learn on the piano. Use the diagram of the piano given in appendix II as a reference:

THE C MAJOR SCALE

C	D	E	F	G	A	B	C
1	2	3	4	5	6	7	8

Psychologically, the C major scale is not satisfactory because it ends short of the goal of completion. That is, the return to the upper

C (no. 8) is not attained. It could be put forward that there are more chakras lying above the crown, and that is where completion does occur. Technically, many people's voices are more comfortable in a range lower than the C major scale tones. If a seven-tone Western scale is chosen for toning, then the pure or natural minor scale beginning on A as suggested by Elizabeth Laurel Keyes,[1] a pioneer in healing with the voice, is preferable, because in addition to being an all-white-key scale, it begins two tones lower than the C major scale, allowing for vocal comfort.

THE A MINOR SCALE

A	B	C	D	E	F	G	A
1	2	3	4	5	6	7	8

Another scale of seven tones, proposed by the late sound healer Kay Gardner and others for chakra toning[2] is the so-called overtone scale. It consists of those frequencies that appear in the fourth octave of an overtone series. Some would say it is the true natural acoustical scale. Gardner starts it on C, investing C as the great fundamental tone, but it could be shifted to another starting note for vocal comfort. It cannot be devoid of sharps or flats no matter what the starting note is, and it is not an easy scale of tones to get into the ear. Here it is starting on C, and also starting on A.*

---

*The symbol "#" stands for a sharp, one-half step higher than the given letter name. The symbol "b" stands for a flat, one half-step lower than the given letter name. In the majority of cases these are represented by the black keys of the piano.

THE OVERTONE SCALE

C	D	E	F#	G	A	Bb	C
A	B	C#	D#	E	F#	G	A
I	2	3	4	5	6	7	8

I have never been satisfied with these three principal seven-note scales, and have pondered what an alternative might be. There was dissatisfaction that the tone C represented the lowest chakra. C in Western music is a tone of centrality, at the heart of things, so to speak. Intuition dictates that is where it belongs—at the heart chakra. The heart corresponds to the air element and so the question was asked: What is the quality of the interval (in musical terms, an interval being the distance between two tones) between the heart and the beginning of the chakras, the root? The source for answering this question was the polarity and sound therapist John Beaulieu, who has created specific tuning forks and categorized their combinations according to the elements.[3] In his system, the principal air elemental interval is the perfect fifth, the distance of five white keys (e.g., C to G, and F to C) on the piano. It is an interval of stability and peace, which Lao-Tzu described as the sound of universal harmony between the forces of yin and yang. If the foundation of the chakras is the root, then proportionally the descent down five tones from C would reveal the root tone, namely F.

DESCENDING WHITE KEY SCALE FROM C TO F

C	B	A	G	F
I	2	3	4	5

Now there were two tones in place. However, this interval proved problematical. The descent was down five tones but the heart is only four places above the root. Eventually a solution revealed itself. What is the most universal scale in the world, used in every culture's folk music and in some cultures' classical music? It is the principal scale for all of the music of China. Namely, the pentatonic or five-tone scale. Beginning on the F, there are only four tones to reach the perfect fifth tone of C. In the illustration below, the F and G are repeated an octave higher to give a seven-tone scale for chakra toning:

THE PENTATONIC SCALE

F	G	A	C	D	F	G
1	2	3	4	5	6	7

This scale is not only universal, but it overcomes the drawbacks of the previous ones. It has already reached completion by the sixth tone, F, corresponding to the brow, which means the higher realms of the brow and crown chakras are in the next dimension of the second octave. Furthermore, it also sets up a relationship between the root (foundation) and the brow (insight), F to F; and the sacral (creative juices) and the crown (higher consciousness), G to G. The scale also provides two further harmonious perfect-fifth intervals between the lower G (sacral/creativity) and the D (throat/communication); and the C (heart/compassion) and the upper G (crown/bliss). Finally, beginning on F, there is a lower range of notes for vocal ease.

Chinese musical theorists have set the foundation tone of their music as F and connect this with the element earth. This gives more support in choosing the pentatonic scale starting on F.

A further point of intuitive verification that F is the right keynote to begin this scale came from a well-known musical source. The root chakra is of the earth element, in other words, of all that stems from the earth and even nature itself. What is the greatest piece of music celebrating nature? Arguably, Beethoven's *Pastoral Symphony*. And in what key did he place this work? F major.

Curiously, some research by Dr. Valerie Hunt also draws attention to one tone in this scale, C. She used EMG (electromyography) electrodes to study bioelectrical variations of skin corresponding to the positions of the chakras, and found regular high frequency, sinusoidal electrical oscillations coming from these points. She reported that the chakras lay in a band of frequencies between 100 and 1600 cycles per second (cps), with the heart going up to about 250 cps.[4] It just so happens that a middle C on the piano in current tuning is 261 cps, and if we alter the tuning system based on C = 1 cps, and keep doubling it, middle C becomes 256, close to the 250 cps.

The letters of the pentatonic scale begin some fundamental appropriate words for describing the chakras:

Chakra	Note Letter	Key Word
Root	F	Foundation
Sacral	G	Genesis
Solar plexus	A	Authority
Heart	C	Compassion
Throat	D	Declaration
Brow	F	Foresight
Crown	G	Godhead

Vowel/Consonant Combinations for Two Chakras

Readers should feel free to experiment with mixing the various vowels and consonants, whereby two different chakra sounds can be joined. The following seed syllables are possible combinations of the different consonants and vowels, with a closing *M* for the purpose of interconnecting two chakras while toning. Where available, a similar-sounding English word is given, though occasionally the sound of *N* replaces *M* in that word, or the *M* is dropped altogether.

LUHM (lumbar)	*VUHM*	*RUHM* (rum)	*YUHM* (yummy)
LOOM (loom)	*VOOM*	*ROOM* (room)	*YOOM*
LOHM (loam)	*VOHM*	*ROHM* (roam)	*YOHM*
LAWM (lawn)	*VAWM*	*RAWM* (raw)	*YAWM* (yawn)

LAHM (lament)	VAHM (vomit)	RAHM	YAHM
LAYM (lame)	VAYM	RAYM (ray)	YAYM
LEHM (lemon)	VEHM (venom)	REHM (remedy)	YEHM (yen)
LIM (lime)	VIM (vine)	RIM (rhyme)	YIM
LIHM (limb)	VIHM (vim)	RIHM (rim)	YIHM
LEEM (lean)	VEEM	REEM (ream)	YEEM
HUHM (hum)	SUHM (sum)	C/KUHM (come)	
HOOM (whom)	SOOM (soon)	C(K)OOM (coo)	
HOHM (home)	SOHM	C(K)OHM (comb)	
HAWM (haw)	SAWM (sawn)	C(K)AWM	
HAHM	SAHM (psalm)	C(K)AHM (calm)	
HAYM	SAYM (same)	C(K)AYM (came)	
HEHM (hem)	SEHM	C(K)EHM (chemist)	
HIM	SIM	C(K)IM	
HIHM (him)	SIHM (simple)	C(K)IHM (kin)	
HEEM	SEEM (seem)	C(K)EEM (keen)	

Symbolic Shapes of the Alphabet

The following commentaries on the alphabet as used in the seed sounds are based on my personal visualizations and are offered as further inspiration in extracting the therapeutic juices of the sounds. One way of making use of these symbolic descriptions is to visualize the shapes or actually look at artistic renderings of the described letters when toning.

L (ROOT)

If two capital letters *L* are placed side by side with one upside down, they form a square. The square with its right angles is a block of solidity, as a cube is like a foundation stone set into the earth. Its four corners correspond to the four petals of the root chakra.

V, U (SACRAL)

The *V* shape has frequently been the symbol of waves and thus water. The *V* and *U* are interrelated as two *V* letters joined together become known as a double *U*. Both the *V* and *U* (*OO*) are like receptacles into which water could be poured or in which something could be incubated. This is especially represented by the woman's womb located in the region of the sacral chakra, and the associative words *vulva* and *uterus*.

O (SOLAR PLEXUS)

The complete roundedness of the *O* is simply a representation of the primary sphere, the sun associated with this chakra. In its seamless circuit it symbolizes a resolution that cannot be broken.

R (SOLAR PLEXUS)

The upper half of the letter *R* is a half circle, which is complementary to its companion solar plexus sound *O*, and represents the torso. Attached to this torso are legs, symbolizing standing firm within our authority.

Y, A (HEART)

Each of these letters, in its way, denotes a trinity, a three-in-oneness. The *Y* with its three spokes radiating from a center point and the *A* as a triangle and three connecting lines. Within all great religions there is the call to "love thy neighbor as thy self," which has to emerge from the heart. Among them are those that portray the Godhead as a trinity, for example, Christianity (Father, Son, and Holy Spirit), and Hinduism (Brahma, Krishna, and Shiva).

H (THROAT)

The *H,* with its two parallel vertical lines joined together by a horizontal one, suggests a duality that is bridged. The two vertical lines are like two "I's" representing two beings who desire to be in union with one another. The chakra of communication is a contributing vehicle for this union to occur.

I (BROW)

Here again there are two small, parallel horizontal lines joined by a larger vertical line. This *I* is the perfect symbol for a human being or *I*ndividual (undivided). The horizontal lines represent the ego and the divine Self and, in order for an individual to become spiritually unified, the ego has to be pure and thus reflect totally that divine Self. The duality becomes nonduality. The insight of the brow chakra can lead us in this direction.

S (BROW)

The letter *S* has a lovely flow to its shape. If that flow were continued to link the end to the beginning, and the letter placed on its side, the result would be the symbol for infinity. To see and go beyond, as in clairvoyance, an attribute of the brow chakra, has this quality of infinitude.

K (CROWN)

The shape of the letter *K* can be seen as an arrow striking a target, as illustrated earlier. In spiritual terms this is a piercing of the final veils of ignorance and knowing permanent liberation.

E (CROWN)

The letter *E* is another form of trinity with its three prongs. Placed with the prongs pointing downward, it becomes a trinity that pushes upward the platform of unity toward *E*ternity. In that position it bears a kind of resemblance to the humming *M,* the greatest vocal sound for knowing spiritual contentment.

Notes

Chapter 1.
Creation as Vibration

1. David Elkington, *In the Name of the Gods* (Sherborne, Dorset, U.K.: Green Man Press, 2001), 199.

2. Dale Pond, *The Physics of Love: The Ultimate Universal Laws* (Santa Fe, N.Mex.: The Message Company, 1996), 16.

3. Steve Connor, "Music of Creation Is Recorded By a Time Machine," *The Independent* (U.K.), April 30, 2001.

4. Prof. Mark Whittle, "Sounds from the Infant Universe," Abstract for talk at AAS session on public outreach, June 6, 2004. Examples of the sounds can be found at www.astro.virginia.edu/dmv8f. The following recordings are of actual and realized planetary music: *Celestial Love Songs* (as detected by the space probes Voyager 1 and 2 of NASA), produced by BrainMind Research, Encinitas, Calif., 1995; and *The Harmony of the World: Realization for the Ear of Johannes Kepler's* Harmonices Mundi (1619), on the Kepler label (www.willie ruff.com).

5. Carolin Crawford, "Discussing Galaxies," *In Our Time*, BBC Radio 4, June 29, 2006.

6. Lynne McTaggert, *The Field* (London: Element Books, 2001), xv–xxiii.

7. Hunbatz Men, *Secrets of Mayan Science/Religion* (Rochester, Vt.: Bear & Company, 1990), 90.

8. Excellent books on this subject are: Hans Jenny, *Cymatics: A Study of Wave Phenomena and Vibration* (Newmarket, N.H.: Macromedia, 2001); Alexander Lauterwasser, *Water Sound Images: The Creative Music of the Universe* (Newmarket, N.H.: Macromedia, 2006); Masaru Emoto, *Messages from Water* (Tokyo: Hado Publishing, 1999).

Chapter 2.
The Nature of the Chakras

1. Harish Johari, *Chakras: Energy Centers of Transformation* (Rochester, Vt.: Destiny Books, 2000), 77.
2. Richard Gerber, *Vibrational Medicine* (Rochester, Vt.: Bear & Company, 2001), 413.
3. Gerber, *Vibrational Medicine*, 393.

Chapter 3.
The Psychology of the Chakras as
Related to Vowels and Consonants

1. Edward Hoffman, *The Hebrew Alphabet: A Mystical Journey* (San Francisco: Chronicle Books, 1998), 18.
2. Hoffman, *The Hebrew Alphabet*, 14.
3. Sri Shymaji Bhatnagar, *Microchakras: Inner Tuning for Psychological Well-Being* (Rochester, Vt.: Inner Traditions, 2009), 5.
4. Don Campbell, Keynote address (International Sound Healing Conference, Santa Fe, N. Mex., November 10, 2006).

Chapter 11.
All Chakras and the Consonant *M*

1. Arden Mahlberg, "Getting the Ego Humming: Therapeutic Application of the Auditory Archetype M," in *Music and Miracles*, Ed. Don Campbell (Adyar, Madras, India: Quest Books, 1992), 210–29.

Chapter 12.
Toning Practices for the Chakras

1. Richard Gerber, *Vibrational Medicine* (Rochester, Vt.: Bear & Company), 414.

2. Georg Feuerstein, *Tantra: The Path of Ecstasy* (Boston: Shambhala South Asia Editions, 1998), 108.

3. Mantak Chia, *Taoist Ways to Transform Stress into Vitality* (Huntington, N.Y.: Healing Tao Books, 1985), 61–64.

4. Hunbatz Men, *Secrets of Mayan Science/Religion* (Rochester, Vt.: Bear & Company, 1990), 82.

Appendix III.
Using a Musical Scale for Toning

1. Laurel Elizabeth Keyes (with Don Campbell), *Toning: The Creative and Healing Power of the Voice* (Camarillo, Calif.: DeVorss Publications, 2008), 87–89.

2. Kay Gardner, *Sounding the Inner Landscape: Music As Medicine* (Stonington, Maine: Caduceus Publications, 1990), 16–24.

3. John Beaulieu, *Music and Sound in the Healing Arts* (Barrytown, N.Y.: Station Hill Press, 1987), 95–97.

4. Richard Gerber, *Vibrational Medicine* (Rochester, Vt.: Bear & Company, 2001), 123.

Recommended Reading

Andrews, Ted. *Sacred Sounds: Transformation through Music & Word*. St. Paul, Minn.: Llewellyn Worldwide, Ltd., 1992.

Baur, Alfred. *Healing Sounds: Fundamentals of Chirophonetics*. Fair Oaks, Calif.: Rudolf Steiner College Press, 1993.

Beaulieu, John. *Music and Sound in the Healing Arts*. Barrytown, N.Y.: Station Hill Press, 1987.

Berendt, Joachim-Ernst. *Nada Brahma: The World Is Sound*. London: East-West Publications Ltd., 1988.

Bhatnagar, Sri Shyamji. *Microchakras: InnerTuning for Psychological Well-Being*. Rochester Vt.: Inner Traditions, 2009.

Brennan, Barbara Ann. *Hands of Light: Guide to Healing through the Human Energy Field*. New York: Bantam Books, 1988.

Campbell, Don, ed. *Music and Miracles*. Wheaton, Ill.: The Theosophical Publishing House, 1992.

Catoire, Jean. *The Phenomenon of Sound*. Unpublished manuscript translated from the French, 1979.

Chia, Mantak. *Taoist Ways to Transform Stress into Vitality*. Huntington, N.Y.: Healing Tao Books, 1985.

Condron, Barbara. *Kundalini Rising: Mastering Creative Energies*. Windyville, Mo.: School of Metaphysics Publishing, 2001.

Cooper, Lyz. *Sounding the Mind of God: Therapeutic Sound for Self-healing and Transformation*. Hampshire, U.K.: O Books, 2009.

D'Angelo, James. *The Healing Power of the Human Voice*. Rochester, Vt.: Healing Arts Press, 2005.

Danielou, Alain. *Sacred Music: Its Origin, Powers, and Future*. Varanasi, India: Indica Books, 2003.

Feinson, Roy. *The Secret Universe of Names: The Dynamic Interplay of Names and Destiny*. Woodstock, N.Y.: Overlook Duckworth, Peter Mayer Publishers, Inc., 2004.

Feuerstein, Georg. *The Shambhala Encyclopedia of Yoga*. Boston: Shambhala Publications, Inc., 1997.

———. *Tantra: The Path of Ecstasy*. Boston: Shambhala South Asia Editions, 1998.

Gardner, Kay. *Sounding the Inner Landscape: Music as Medicine*. Stonington, Maine: Caduceus Publications, 1990.

Gerber, Richard. *Vibrational Medicine,* 3rd ed. Rochester, Vt.: Bear & Co., 2001.

Godwin, Joscelyn. *The Mystery of the Seven Vowels in Theory and Practice*. Grand Rapids, Mich.: Phanes Press, 1991.

Goldman, Jonathan. *The Divine Name: The Sound that Can Change the World*. Carlsbad, Calif.: Hay House, 2010.

Goldman, Jonathan, and Andi Goldman. *Tantra of Sound: How to Enhance Intimacy with Healing*. Charlottesville, Va.: Hampton Roads, 2005.

Hoffman, Edward. *The Hebrew Alphabet: A Mystical Journey*. San Francisco: Chronicle Books, 1998.

Johari, Harish. *Chakras: Energy Centers of Transformation*. Rochester, Vt.: Destiny Books, 2000.

Judith, Anodea. *Wheels of Life: A User's Guide to the Chakra System*. Woodbury, Minn.: Llewellyn Publications, 2007.

Keyes, Laurel Elizabeth, with Don Campbell. *Toning: The Creative and Healing Power of the Voice* (with CD). Camarillo, Calif.: DeVorss Publications, 2008.

Khanna, Madhu. *Yantra: The Tantric Symbol of Cosmic Unity*. London: Thames & Hudson, 1979.

Kumar, Ravindra. *Kundalini for Beginners: The Shortest Path to Self Realization*. St. Paul, Minn.: Llewellyn Publications, 2000.

Leadbeater, C.W. *The Chakras*. Wheaton, Ill.: The Theosophical Publishing House, 1977.

Lewis, Robert C. *The Sacred Word and its Creative Overtones*. Oceanside, Calif.: The Rosicrucian Fellowship, 1986.

Maman, Fabien. *The Tao of Sound: Acoustic Sound Healing for the 21st Century*. Malibu, Calif.: Tama-Do, The Academy of Sound, Color, and Movement, 2008.

Man, John. *Alpha Beta: How Our Alphabet Shaped the World*. London: Transworld Publishers, 2000.

McClellan, Randall. *The Healing Forces of Music: History, Theory, and Practice*. Lincoln, Neb.: iUniverse, 2000.

McIntosh, Solveig. *Hidden Faces of Ancient Indian Song*. Aldershot, U.K.: Ashgate Publishing Ltd., 2005.

McTaggart, Lynne. *The Field*. London: Element Books, 2001.

Men, Hunbatz. *Secrets of Mayan Science/Religion*. Rochester, Vt.: Bear & Company, 1990.

Mercier, Patricia. *Chakras: Balance Your Energy Flow for Health and Harmony*. London: Godsfield Press Ltd., 2000.

Paul, Russill. *The Yoga of Sound: Healing & Enlightenment through the Practice of Mantra*. Novato, Calif.: New World Library, 2004.

Pond, Dale. *The Physics of Love: The Ultimate Universal Laws*. Santa Fe, N.Mex.: The Message Company, 1996.

Rael, Joseph. *Being and Vibration*. Tulsa, Okla.: Council Oak Books, 1993.

Remen, Rachel Naomi. *My Grandfather's Blessings: Stories of Strength, Refuge, and Belonging*. N.Y.: Riverhead Books, 2000.

Rendel, Peter. *Introduction to the Chakras*. Northamptonshire, U.K.: The Aquarian Press, 1979.

Shola Arewa, Caroline. *Way of the Chakras*. London: Thorsons, 2001.

Shumsky, Susan G. *Exploring Chakras: Awaken your Untapped Energy.* Franklin Lakes, N.J.: The Career Press, Inc., 2000.

Steiner, Rudolf. *Creative Speech: The Nature of Speech Formation.* London: Rudolf Steiner Press, 1978.

Stewart, R. J. *Music Power Harmony.* London: Blandford (Cassell Books), 1990.

Tigunait, Pandit Rajmani. *The Power of Mantra & The Mystery of Initiation.* Honesdale, Pa.: The Himalayan International Institute of Yoga, 1996.

White, Ruth. *Working with Your Chakras.* London: Judy Piatkus Publishers Ltd., 1993.

Whone, Herbert. "The Power of Language: The Inner Meaning of Vowels and Consonants." *Caduceus Magazine UK,* no. 23 (1994), 20–23.

CD Directory

The length of each track is between 1:00 minute and 1:35. Total running time is 66:36 minutes.

❁ PREPARATORY EXERCISE

Track 1. Opening the throat: *GUNG GANG GING* (see page 87)

❁ TONING WITH VOWELS (PAGES 60–66)

Track 2. Root *UH* at 40 bpm on the tone F

Track 3. Sacral *OO* at 48 bpm on the tone G

Track 4. Solar plexus *OH* at 60 bpm on the tone A

Track 5. Solar plexus *AW* at 60 bpm on the tone A

Track 6. Heart *AH* at 72 bpm on the tone C

Track 7. Throat *EH* at 84 bpm on the tone D

Track 8. Throat *AY* at 84 bpm on the tone D

Track 9. Brow *I* at 96 bpm on the tone F (an octave above the root)

Track 10. Brow *IH* at 96 bpm on the tone F (an octave above the root)

Track 11. Crown *EE* at 108 bpm on the tone G (an octave above the sacral)

Notes

- The abbreviation "bpm" stands for "beats per minute" as measured on a musical metronome. These speeds need not be followed. If the speeds are either too slow or too fast for your breath, choose your own speed. A moderate one would be 60 bpm or 72 bpm. Remember that once the sound is brought inside you, a different speed might appear from the one you have chosen. Go with the flow of the inner pulsation.

- The vowels are presented with changing notes moving up through the pentatonic scale, explained in appendix III (page 93). It is not essential to adhere to this rising scale. Either choose a different tone for each chakra according to your intuition, or select one comfortable tone for all the chakras.

- For the given tones, use the keyboard diagram (page 91) in appendix II as a guide.

- The use of the breath aspect three or four times at the end is optional.

- These are condensed examples. Durations are at your discretion. Because of the shortness of these examples, the suggested decrease in volume, as you get close to moving into the inner pulsating sound, is not used.

❀ TONING WITH CONSONANTS

Track 12. Root chakra *L* (page 67)

Track 13. Sacral chakra *V* (page 69)

Track 14. Solar plexus chakra *R* (page 70)

Track 15. Heart chakra *Y* (page 71)

Track 16. Throat chakra *H* (page 73)

Track 17. Brow chakra *S* (page 74)

Track 18. Crown chakra *K* (page 75)

Track 19. All chakras *M* (page 78)

Notes

- The pulsating speeds for *L, V, R,* and *M* can be altered according to your intuition.
- It is not necessary to adhere to the tones used for *L, V, R,* and *M.* Choose any comfortable tone.
- These are condensed versions. The durations of sounding these rituals are at your discretion.
- For the *L, V,* and *R* rituals, two sequences are given of full voice, sliding voice (not *V*), and covered voice.

❀ TONING WITH SEED SYLLABLES

Original Tantra Version Using Only the Tone C

Track 20. Root chakra *LAM*

Track 21. Sacral chakra *VAM*

Track 22. Solar plexus chakra *RAM*

Track 23. Heart chakra *YAM*

Track 24. Throat chakra *HAM*

Track 25. Brow chakra *OM*

Track 26. Crown chakra *MMM*

*Original Tantra Version Using
the Tones of the Pentatonic Scale*

Track 27. Root chakra *LAM* on the tone F

Track 28. Sacral chakra *VAM* on the tone G

Track 29. Solar plexus chakra *RAM* on the tone A

Track 30. Heart chakra *YAM* on the tone C

Track 31. Throat chakra *HAM* on the tone D

Track 32. Brow chakra *OM* on the tone F
(an octave above the root F)

Track 33. Crown chakra *MMM* on the tone G
(an octave above the sacral G)

Adapted Western Version Using Only the Tone C

Track 34. Root chakra *LUHM*

Track 35. Sacral chakra *VOOM*

Track 36. Solar plexus chakra *RAWM*

Track 37. Heart chakra *YAM*

Track 38. Throat chakra *HAYM*

Track 39. Brow chakra *SIM*

Track 40. Crown chakra *KEEM*

Adapted Western Version Using the Tones of the Pentatonic Scale

Track 41. Root chakra *LUHM* on the tone F

Track 42. Sacral chakra *VOOM* on the tone G

Track 43. Solar plexus chakra *RAWM* on the tone A

Track 44. Heart chakra *YAM* on the tone C

Track 45. Throat chakra *HAYM* on the tone D

Track 46. Brow chakra *SIM* on the tone F
(an octave above the root F)

Track 47. Crown chakra *KEEM* on the tone G
(an octave above the sacral G)

Notes

- The speed of the repetitions can be slightly slower or faster than given. As with the vowels and consonants, the durations are at your discretion.

- For the given tones, use the keyboard diagram (page 91) in appendix II as a guide.

Index